Caves of Enlightenment

Caves of Enlightenment

Proceedings
of the
American Schools of Oriental Research
Dead Sea Scrolls Jubilee Symposium

(1947–1997)

Edited by
James H. Charlesworth

BIBAL Press
North Richland Hills, Texas

BIBAL Press
An imprint of D. & F. Scott Publishing, Inc.
P.O. Box 821653
N. Richland Hills, TX 76182
1–888–788–2280
bibal@cmpu.net
www.cmpu.net/public/bibal

Printed in the United States of America

02 01 00 99 98   5 4 3 2 1

Library of Congress Cataloging-in-Publication Data

Dead Sea Scrolls Jubilee Symposium (1997 : Napa (Calif.))
    Caves of enlightenment : proceedings of the American Schools of
Oriental Research Dead Sea Scrolls Jubilee Symposium (1947-1997) / edited
by J.H. Charlesworth.
        p. cm.
    Conference held Nov. 20, 1997 in Napa, Calif.
    Includes bibliographical references and index.

    ISBN 0-94-103768-1 (pbk.)
    1. Dead Sea scrolls--Congresses. I. Charlesworth, James H. II.
American Schools of Oriental Research. III. Title.
    BM487 .A86 1998
    296.1'55--ddc21
                                            98-25408
                                            CIP

Cover by KC Scott

Dedicated to the memory of

Jean Hamilton Charlesworth

that lively Scottish lassie, who zoomed through the Negev with the likes of Nelson Glueck—my mother, who passed away on August 19, 1998, and who will always beam so brightly from the Pitt Yearbook. She was my first Bible teacher and is the one to whom the Albright Annual Professor's apartment is dedicated. She experienced this book proleptically, but now she will never read it.

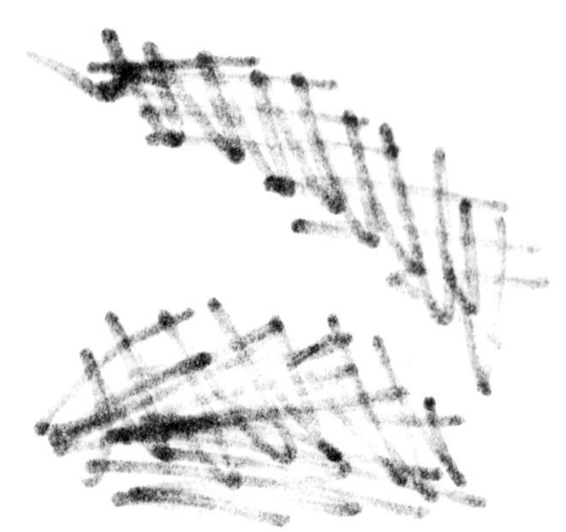

Publication of this volume
has been sponsored by
The Foundation for Biblical Archaeology
and
The Foundation on Judaism and Christian Origins.

Contents

Preface   xi

Abbreviations   xvii

J. A. Sanders
   The Judaean Desert Scrolls and the
   History of the Text of the Hebrew Bible   1

M. Broshi
   Was Qumran, Indeed, a Monastery? The
   Consensus and Its Challengers, an
   Archaeologist's View   19

S. White Crawford
   How Archaeology Affects the Study of Texts:
   Reflections on the Category "Rewritten Bible"
   at Qumran   39

D. Dimant
   Dualism at Qumran: New Perspectives   55

J. H. Charlesworth
   John the Baptizer, Jesus, and the Essenes   75

J. D. G. Dunn
   Paul and the Dead Sea Scrolls   105

Indices   129

Preface

In 1947, perhaps in the spring, Bedouin discovered leather manuscripts in a cave to the northwest of the Dead Sea. The manuscripts had been hidden by priests just before Jericho and Jerusalem were destroyed by the Roman army two millennia ago. In late 1997, three major conferences celebrated the jubilee of this monumental discovery. The first was in Jerusalem, and the second in Princeton. The third was the American Schools of Oriental Research celebration in the Napa Valley. This book contains the proceedings of that symposium.

Not long after the discovery of the Dead Sea Scrolls, some were brought to the ASOR on Saladin Street in Jerusalem. Fortunately, in residence was a young scholar who was also a gifted photographer. He photographed the large Isaiah scroll, and, on February 25, 1948, sent an airletter with photographs to William F. Albright, one of the leading archaeologists and paleographers in the world. Here is the full text of Albright's letter:

March 8th, 1948

Dear Trever,

Your air-letter of Feb. 25th, with its enclosures, arrived this morning and I immediately got out my magnifying glass and started in. I am now having the prints enlarged so I can study the script to better advantage. My heartiest congratulations on the greatest MS discovery of modern times! There is no doubt whatever in my mind that the script is more archaic than that of the Nash Papyrus, standing very close to that of the third-century Egyptian papyri and ostraca in Aramaic.[1] Of course, in the present state of our definite knowledge about Hebrew paleography it would be safe only to date it in the Maccabean period, i.e., not later than the accession of Herod the Great. I should prefer a date around 100 BC. The script is in every respect older than that of the Dura parchment fragment.

1   Albright corrected the spelling of papyri by hand.

[The following is prefaced by Albright with these words within his parentheses:]

(continued from outside.)

     In my excitement I began writing on the wrong side of the sheet! I repeat that in my opinion you have made the greatest MS discovery of modern times—certainly the greatest biblical MS find. The spelling is most interesting, resembling that of the Nash Papyrus very closely[2] The tendency to hyper-correction in writing כי as כיא is most extraordinary. Burrows will now have a chance to forget the events in Palestine for a while. Let us hope that nothing happens to your precious finds!

     I don't anticipate any very significant textual corrections of the text of Isaiah, but the new material will revolutionize our conception of the development of Hebrew orthography. And who knows what treasures may be concealed in the remaining rolls!

     It is a very fine thing that you have been able to get such an important result as this discovery from your difficult year in Jerusalem. You can imagine how my eyes bulged when I saw the script through my magnifying glass! What an absolutely incredible find![3] And there can happily not be the slightest doubt in the world about the genuineness of the MS.

Cordially,

[signed W. F. Albright]

P.S. I shall keep the business of this MS very quiet.

The letter was addressed to the following:

Professor John C. Trever,
American School of Oriental Research,
Jerusalem,
Palestine

2   There is no punctuation at the end of this sentence.
3   Albright became so excited that he mistyped two words (absolutely and incredible) but corrected them by hand.

Above the address is handwritten "Arrived March 15." The letter was mailed from Baltimore, Maryland, on March 8 and is stamped at 12 P.M.[4]

The atypical redundancy, the repetitive exclamations, the cluster of typos, as well as Albright's beginning the letter on "the first fold" of the airletter, placard the understandable excitement he felt. His expressions and assessment are truly amazing. He had it right, almost perfectly dating the Great Isaiah Scroll without good photographs. His dating of this Hebrew manuscript to the Maccabean period was rejected by some scholars; they foolishly claimed that the scrolls were medieval.

Albright's paleographical dating of the Great Isaiah Scroll has been vindicated. In 1994, the Isaiah Scroll was dated to the second century BCE by Carbon 14 analysis (AMS C-14). It is a pity that some so-called Qumran experts never mastered, and even today disparage, paleography.

The ASOR remained in the forefront of Dead Sea Scrolls Research. The first edition of the *Rule of the Community* was published by the ASOR; it was edited by Millar Burrows, who had been director of the ASOR but away when Trever photographed the scrolls. He called the document the *Manual of Discipline*, because it reminded him of the Methodist work by that name. Thanks to the ASOR, other scrolls also soon appeared in diplomatic editions, with photographs and transcriptions. It is a pity that all the Dead Sea Scrolls were not printed so efficiently, so inexpensively, and so accurately.

Burrows shifted his research to the Dead Sea Scrolls—as Albright had imagined. He published two volumes that were the first collection of translations and introductions to the Dead Sea Scrolls. William Brownlee, who was a fellow at the ASOR when the first scrolls were brought to the ASOR, became interested in the *Rule of the Community* and the *Habakkuk Pesher*, both of which were photographed by Trever in the basement of the ASOR. Brownlee published translations of each scroll with copious notes. Both works appeared as ASOR publications. Brownlee

---

4   For photographs of both sides of the airletter, see A. Schick, O. Betz, and F. M. Cross, *Jesus und die Schriftrollen von Qumran* (Berneck: Schwengeler Verlag, 1996) p. 16.

also offered the first course on the Dead Sea Scrolls; it was at Duke University.

Reading Albright's letter might give one the impression that since he accurately assessed the importance and antiquity of the Dead Sea Scrolls that the matter was settled. Scholars and institutions of higher learning, however, were too dubious. The large scrolls found in Cave 1 that had been studied at the ASOR were taken to the USA for sale. Neither Duke University nor other universities that had them on public display and could have purchased them obtained even one scroll. And all could have been purchased for merely $250,000. Perhaps that was because of uncertainty as to their value; it was also assuredly related to their legal status and the emotions generated by the establishment of Israel in 1948.

In the *Times* of April 12, 1948, appeared the following blurb:

> [New York, April 11]
>
> Yale University announced yesterday the discovery in Palestine of the earliest known manuscript of the Book of Isaiah. It was found in the Syrian monastery of St. Mark in Jerusalem, where it had been preserved in a scroll of parchment dating to about the first century BC. Recently it was identified by scholars of the American School of Oriental Research at Jerusalem.

There were also examined at the school three other ancient Hebrew scrolls. One was part of a commentary on the Book of Habakkuk; another seemed to be a manual of discipline of some comparatively little known sect or monastic order, possibly the Essenes. The third scroll has not been identified.[5]

This oldest newspaper announcement rightly highlighted the pioneering work of the ASOR, but the report is erroneous. The Dead Sea Scrolls were not discovered in St. Mark's Monastery. The Bedouin brought them from the cave and up out of the Judean desert to Kando in Bethlehem. This Syrian Orthodox Christian brought them to his bishop, Athanasius Yeshue

---

5   For a photograph, see Schick, et al., *Jesus und die Schriftrollen*, p. 18.

Samuel, who was in the Old City of Jerusalem. He knew the scrolls were not written in Syriac, as Kando had surmised. To test his hypothesis that the script was an ancient form of Hebrew, Bishop Samuel had them taken to the ASOR on Saladin Street for examination. It was at the ASOR, just north of the old walls of Jerusalem, that the scrolls were first studied seriously. Albright's genius revealed the authenticity and antiquity of the scrolls. These scrolls found to the northwest of the Dead Sea are biblical and parabiblical works in Hebrew, and they antedate the time of Hillel and Jesus.

The unidentified scroll, according to the Times, led some specialists to imagine that the long-lost apocryphon of Lamech had been recovered. Eventually, the scroll was given a new name. It was called the *Genesis Apocryphon*.

In the first half of this century, only a mound of dirt separated the ASOR, now renamed the Albright Institute, from the Ecole Biblique. The biblical specialists at the two archaeological schools have always been close neighbors, so it is understandable that a strong personal relationship developed between William Albright and Roland de Vaux. I experienced this relationship myself in late winter 1968, as Albright and de Vaux, encircled by a group of younger scholars, conversed at a table in the Ecole Biblique's lounge. The erudite conversation was as amicable as it was animated.

This cordial relationship continued as specialists at the ASOR and Ecole Biblique worked cooperatively on the Dead Sea Scrolls. Thanks to the leadership of these two schools, which was enriched by Eleazar Sukenik's insights,[6] a consensus emerged regarding the Dead Sea Scrolls. They were pre-Christian and Jewish. The men who lived at Qumran near the caves owned the scrolls, copied some of them, composed others, and hid them in caves during the First Jewish War against Rome. The Qumranites were identified as a strict form of the Essenes. The scrolls were important for understanding the shaping of the Hebrew

---

6   See Sukenik's emotional response, somewhat like that of Albright's, but with a justifiable and understandable pride in the re-establishment of the State of Israel, see Y. Yadin, *The Message of the Scrolls*, edited by Charlesworth (Christian Origins Library; New York: Crossroad, 1992).

Bible and for clarifying the Jewish origins of Christianity. The members of the two schools joined forces in excavating Cave 1 for fourteen days in early 1949,[7] and then they launched the task of publishing the Dead Sea Scrolls.

As I look back through the mists to the origins of Qumran research, I see great giants moving about on the earth, as if שטן שמיא לארעא נחת (4Q530, col. 2, line 16). Along with others, then young and impressionistic, I stood in awe of Albright and de Vaux, and those like Kathleen Kenyon and Nelson Glueck who moved in and about our discussions. Even today, I side with those who think reverently about the great ones, the forefathers who were wise in instruction.[8]

The following essays salute the involvement of the ASOR in Dead Sea Scrolls research, and celebrate the monumental achievements made possible because of the discovery of a library from the time of Hillel and Jesus. The first author is a member of the original Dead Sea Scrolls Editorial Team, and the second the first Curator of the Shrine of the Book. The third and fourth essays are by gifted women; one is an American who has been drawing attention to the "Rewritten Bible" at Qumran; the other is an Israeli who has focused her research on Qumran theology. The final two essays are by the editor of the first critical and comprehensive edition of the Dead Sea Scrolls, and by a British scholar who is a specialist on Paul.

J. H. Charlesworth
1998–1999 Annual Professor
Albright Institute

---

7   See W. Baumgartner, "Die ältesten Texte des Alten Testaments," *Die Weltwoche* 17. Jahrgang/Nr. 830 (7 October 1949) 7. In Schick, et al., *Jesus und die Schriftrollen*, p. 19, see the photograph of de Vaux with Lancaster Harding, the Antiquities Authority, in Cave 1 in which were found 71 fragments. But no less than 56 jars had been hidden in this cave.

8   Sirach 44:4.

Abbreviations

AB	Anchor Bible Commentary Series
ANRW	*Aufsieg und Niedergang der römischen Welt*. ed. H. Tempori and W. Haase, Berlin, 1972.
Ant	Josephus, *The Jewish Antiquities*
ASOR	The American Schools of Oriental Research
BA	*Biblical Archaeologist*
BARev	*Biblical Archaeological Review*
BHQ	*Biblia Hebraica Quinta*
BHS	*Biblia Hebraica Stuttgartensia*
BJRL	*Bulletin of the John Rylands University Library of Manchester*
BYU	Brigham Young University
BZ	*Biblische Zeitschrift*
CBQ	*Catholic Biblical Quarterly*
CRAIBL	*Comptes rendus de l'Académie des inscriptions et belles-lettres*
CSCO	Corpus scriptorum christianorum orientalium
CTAT	*Critique textuelle de l'Ancien Testament*
DJD	Discoveries in the Judean Desert (Oxford: Clarendon Press 1955–)
EncJud	*Encyclopedia Judaica* (1971)
FRLANT	Forshungen zur Religion und Literatur des Alten und Neuen Testaments
HOTTP	Hebrew Old Testament Text Project of the United Bible Societies
HUB	*Hebrew University Bible*
HUBP	Hebrew University Bible Project
IOS	*Israel Oriental Studies*
JANES	*Journal of the Ancient Near Eastern Society of Columbia University*, New York
JBL	*Journal of Biblical Literature*
JJS	*Journal of Jewish Studies*
JNES	*Journal of Near Eastern Studies*
JPS	Jewish Publication Society
JQR	*Jewish Quarterly Review*

ABBREVIATIONS

JSNTsup	*Journal for the Study of the New Testament*: Supplement Series
JSP	*Journal for the Study of the Pseudepigrapha*
JSPSup	*Journal for the Study of the Pseudepigrapha*: Supplement Series
JTS	*Journal of Theological Studies*, Oxford
Jub	*Jubilees*
KEK	Kritisch-Exegetischer Kommentar
LCL	Loeb Classical Library
LXX	Septuagint
MMT (4QMMT)	4QHalackhic Letter=More Precepts of the Torah
MT	Masoretic Text
Nat. Hist.	Pliny the Elder, *Historia Naturalis*
NTa	NeuTestamentliche Abhandlungen
NTS	*New Testament Studies*
RHPR	*Revue d'histoire et philosphie religieuses*, Strasbourg
RQ	*Revue de Qumran*
SAOC	Studies in Ancient Oriental Civilizations
SBL	Society of Biblical Literature
ScrHie	*Scripta Hierosolymitana*
Sem	*Semitica*
SNTSMS	Society for New Testament Studies: Monograph Series
STDJ	Studies on the Texts of the Desert of Judah
SUNT	Studien zur Umwelt des Neuen Testaments
SVTP	Studia in Veteris Testamenti Pseudepigrapha
UBS	United Bible Societies
VT	*Vetus Testamentum*
VTsup	*Vetus Testamentum*: Supplement Series
War	Josephus, *The Jewish Wars*
WBC	World Bible Commentary
WTJ	*Westminster Theological Journal*
WUNT	Wissenschaftliche Untersuchungen zum Neuen Testament
ZDPV	*Zeitschrift des deutschen Palästina-Vereins*
ZTK	*Zeitschrift für Theologie und Kirche*

The Judaean Desert Scrolls and the History of the Text of the Hebrew Bible

James A. Sanders

The title announced for this presentation may be understood as the broad rubric under which I wish to share some thoughts about the impact of the Judaean Desert Scrolls on our current understanding of the history of the text of the Hebrew Bible. It seemed to me appropriate to offer a perspective on that history at the annual meeting of the ASOR, celebrating the fiftieth anniversary of the discovery of Qumran Cave 1, because of the role the ASOR has played from the beginning, both in critical study and publication of the biblical scrolls from the eleven Qumran caves.

While scholars identified with other archaeological schools have made major contributions to the study of the biblical scrolls found among the Judaean Desert Scrolls, there can be little dispute that scholars associated with the ASOR have been especially prominent in publication and critical study of the biblical texts. One thinks of Claremont colleagues, William Brownlee and John Trever, who from the beginning were responsible for recognizing, photographing and, in Brownlee's case, assessing the value of the large Isaiah Scroll from Cave 1, as well as the biblical text of the Habakkuk Commentary. It is certainly appropriate at this time to recognize again the crucial contributions of Frank Moore Cross and Patrick William Skehan, to whom were assigned the lion's share of the biblical fragments from Cave 4. And it is my privilege once more to express my personal gratitude to Cross, Skehan, and John Strugnell for their early scrutiny of my own effort to study and publish the *editio princeps* of the Psalms Scroll from Cave 11. If one went on also to recognize the work of the students of that first generation of American scrolls scholars, the list would expand beyond the limits of time and space of the present assignment.

I was honored when the editors of the *Hebrew University Bible* asked me to join them last July in Jerusalem to offer a perspective on the work of the Hebrew University Bible Project (HUBP) on the history of the text of the Hebrew Bible. After forty years of labor by members of the HUBP and their assistants, *The Book of Isaiah* appeared in its entirety in 1995, and just now this past June, *The Book of Jeremiah*.

The perspective from which I reviewed the work of the HUBP was that of participation on the United Bible Societies' Hebrew Old Testament Text Project (HOTTP), of which I have been a member since its inception in 1969, as well as my own personal work on the history of the text of the Masoretic Psalter.

When viewed in terms of the history of textual criticism since the sixteenth century, the concept underlying the HUBP has been revolutionary. The HOTTP independently joined the HUBP in that revolution. The two projects had quite different needs out of which they separately grew, but they converged in concept as the independent work on each progressed. Both projects are issuing critical editions of the Hebrew Bible—the *Hebrew University Bible* (*HUB*), of which we now have two impressive volumes; and *Biblia*

Hebraica Quinta (*BHQ*), which is scheduled to be published in the year 2002, with fascicles appearing intermittently in advance. The first fascicle, *The Five Scrolls*, should appear next summer in time for the Oslo meeting of the IOSOT.

The HUBP came into being because of the perceived necessity to locate the newly recovered Aleppo Codex in the history of development of the text of the Hebrew Bible. The HOTTP came into being because of the perceived necessity to assist national translation committees around the world in dealing with difficult passages, which often had conflicting solutions in the translations in the colonial or common western languages resorted to by the local translation committees. Because the HOTTP committee was formed by Eugene Nida, the world renowned linguist who headed the translations department of the UBS, its members were selected in large part because of their awareness of the changes being effected in the concept and practice of text criticism by the recovery of the Judaean Desert Scrolls. Results from the study of the scrolls have profoundly affected both projects.

The chief result of the study of the Judaean scrolls for text criticism has been a completely new appreciation of the history of transmission of the biblical text.[1] That history

---

1   See the introduction to Moshe Goshen-Gottstein, *The Hebrew University Bible Project: The Book of Isaiah, Sample Edition with Introduction* (Jerusalem: Magnes, 1965) pp. 11–20; essentially reprinted in M. Goshen-Gottstein, ed., *The Hebrew University Bible: The Book of Isaiah* (Jerusalem: Magnes Press, 1995) pp. xi-xx; extensively edited in *The Hebrew University Bible: The Book of Jeremiah*, ed. by C. Rabin, S. Talmon, E. Tov, eds., (Jerusalem: Magnes, 1997) pp. ix-xiii. See also Shemaryahu Talmon, "Aspects of the Textual Transmission of the Bible in the Light of Qumran Manuscripts," *Textus* 4 (1964) pp. 95–132, and Talmon, "The Old Testament Text," in *The Cambridge History of the Bible*, Vol. 1 (Cambridge: University Press, 1970) pp. 159–99, esp. pp. 164–66; and Dominique Barthélemy, "Text, Hebrew, History of," *Interpreter's Dictionary of the*

is the only ground upon which a valid and responsible hermeneutic of text criticism should be established.[2] While the terminology used by the two projects is slightly different, the history perceived is the same. The discovery of the scrolls and the recovery of Codex Aleppensis provided both the near beginnings of the history of textual transmission and the near climax of its development in the hands of the Ben Asher family at the end of the ninth century CE and the beginning of the tenth. It was now possible to look at that history with a kind of confidence never before experienced in the annals of text criticism.[3]

The HOTTP decided early on that a clear distinction should be made between the history of the literary formation of the text and the subsequent history of the transmission of the text. While those two histories overlap somewhat, it became clear that text criticism had become servile to the particular hermeneutic of exegesis out of which this or that scholar worked. A received reading would sometimes be condemned as corrupt in order for the scholar to construct a different text to fit what the scholar thought the text should have said; then would begin the search for a "variant reading" in the versions, or in Kennicott and de Rossi, to substantiate the new reading. And if such could not be found, then conjecture filled the bill. This view of text criticism still prevails in some circles as can still be seen in commentaries and translations published in the second half of this century. The New English

Bible, Supplementary Volume (Nashville: Abingdon, 1976) pp. 878–84.

2   J. A. Sanders, "Hermeneutics of Text Criticism," *Textus* 18 (1995) pp. 1–26.

3   The work of E. Tov on the Qumran system or practice, especially in orthography, morphology, and scribal practices has been especially helpful; see E. Tov, *Textual Criticism of the Hebrew Bible* (Minneapolis: Fortress, 1992), esp. pp. 100–17.

Bible (1970), The New American Bible (1970), the Bible de Jerusalem[1] (1970), the New Revised Standard Version (1989), and even somewhat the Tanakh (published by the JPS in 1988), provide examples of translations built in part on the older view of text criticism. The older Revised Standard Version remained basically true to the King James Version as a formal equivalence translation. HUBP, HOTTP and its offspring, *BHQ,* reject conjecture as a valid text critical choice unless such a conjectural reading can be shown to have been the ancient cause of subsequent disparate readings; but such cases are rare.

The history of transmission of the text begins with the earliest attested texts available, and that aspect of the history has been greatly advanced because of the discovery of the Judaean scrolls. That marks what the HUBP calls the first stage of the history which begins with the third-century BCE fragments from Qumran Cave 4, and with the earliest available Greek translations. Its main characteristic is textual fluidity—limited fluidity to be sure, but nonetheless quite distinct from the second stage. That fluidity, which Goshen-Gottstein saw continuing in a greatly reduced mode into the masoretic period, he called a "main current" with "rivulets" running alongside (see the Isaiah volume, p. xvii), but which Talmon calls "dominant family" and "variant traditions" (Jeremiah volume, p. xii).

The UBS committee calls the stage of a retrojected *Urtext* the First Period, and the stage of earliest attested texts the Second Period—with the clear understanding that the First Period is the province of exegesis, literary criticism, and historical reconstruction, but not that of text criticism.[4] The HUBP, perhaps wisely, sees the history of

---

4   See the trenchant discussion of the blurred distinctions between "higher" and "lower" criticism in Talmon's "Textual Study of the Bible" in *Qumran and the History of the Biblical Text*, F. Cross and S. Talmon, eds., (Cambridge: Harvard University Press, 1975) pp. 327–32.

transmission starting only with the period of the earliest attested texts, their First Stage and our Second Period. We decided to call the period of the literary development, or history of formation of the text, the First Period, toward the end of which textual transmission was admittedly already a part of the picture, so that the two should not be confused.

There is then a clear demarcation between biblical manuscripts that fit the first stage and those that date from after the fall of Jerusalem—by and large, the distinction between biblical texts from Qumran and those from the other provenances covered by the general term, Judaean Desert Scrolls. These latter (Murabba'at, Ḥever, Masada) fit a proto-MT pattern we already knew in the quite literal Greek translations attributed to Aquila, Theodotion, and, to some extent, Symmachus, which date from early in the second century CE. The location of the Greek Minor Prophets Scroll from Naḥal Ḥever in the late first century BCE, or early first century CE, provided the clear link necessary to see that the first century of the Common Era was one of intensive textual stabilization which resulted in a standard which would be called proto-masoretic.[5]

In summation, the Judaean Desert Scrolls have provided the base for the new history of transmission of the biblical text. The link in the transition from pre-masoretic to proto-masoretic thus came to light and became an essential part of the history of the text as now perceived. The shift from pre- to proto-masoretic is rather dramatic to observe, though "thin layers" of variant readings continue even into citations in rabbinic literature, and can be seen in the work of Jerome in the fourth and early fifth century CE. At the other end of the spectrum, it has become clear for many of us (*pace* Paolo Sacchi and the Turin School) that the variant

---

5   D. Barthélemy, *Les Devanciers d'Aquila*, VTSup 10 (Leiden: E. J. Brill, 1963); *The Greek Minor Prophets Scroll from Nahal Hever* (8HevXIIgr), ed. by E. Tov, DJD 8 (Oxford: Clarendon, 1990) pp. ix-x, 1–2.

readings in post-eleventh century masoretic manuscripts collated by Kennicott, de Rossi, and Ginsburg were derivative and, with a few exceptions, do not have readings that pierce back before the masoretic period.[6]

The HUBP plans publishing text critical commentaries later to accompany the fascicles of the *HUB*,[7] whereas the HOTTP has published elaborate text critical commentaries authored by Dominique Barthélemy in *Critique textuelle de l'Ancien Testament*, three hefty volumes of which (of a total of six projected) have already appeared.[8] Each fascicle of *BHQ* will be accompanied by a succinct text critical commentary.

Articles in *Textus* and elsewhere, written by members of the HUBP, stress the importance of bringing medieval rabbinic and Qaraite grammarians and commentators into text critical discussions. Each problem dealt with by the HOTTP, as seen in *CTAT*, includes the medieval Jewish and Qaraite sources in its discussion of the textual history of each problem. And often we found that the medieval grammarians' knowledge of Biblical Hebrew and Aramaic grammar and syntax, the philological tools and grammatical theories which they learned from grammarians of the Arabic language rather than from Greek and Latin classical grammarians (as is the case with modern European Hebrew grammars) offered the key to understand the textual problem addressed. Apparatus V-VI in *HUB* provides a bare beginning of such a commentary for the books of Isaiah and Jeremiah, but there can be no substitute for a text critical commentary to accompany each biblical book, as is planned also for *BHQ*.

---

6   M. Goshen-Gottstein, "Hebrew Biblical Manuscripts: Their History and Their Place in the HUBP Edition," *Biblica* 48 (1967) pp. 243–90.

7   See the sample offered by S. Talmon and E. Tov, "A Commentary on the Text of Jeremiah 1. The LXX of Jeremiah 1:1–7," *Textus* 9 (1981) pp. 1–15.

8   D. Barthélemy, *Critique textuelle de l'Ancien Testament*, Vols. 1–3 (Fribourg: Presses universitaires, 1982, 1986, 1992).

The *HUB* offers two distinct innovations which are very important. I know of no prior effort in a text edition to cover Scripture citations in the basic rabbinic literature: Mishnah, Tosefta, the two Talmudim and the great Midrashim. The importance of this will only gradually be seen by some students of the text. As the editors carefully state, this is a delicate area which requires knowledge of the rabbinic mind to evaluate, but it certainly belongs in a critical edition of the text which claims to provide in its apparatuses a succinct, but complete, history of the text of the Bible. If pre-masoretic readings survive into the proto-masoretic period we need to know it, even if the "rivulets" or "thin layers" have considerably diminished in number. Citations in rabbinic literature demonstrate clearly the adaptability of the Masoretic Text even within rather clear-cut limits of manipulability. Scripture in the NT is virtually ignored in the *HUB*. Some formulaic citations of Scripture in the NT, especially in Matthew and Luke, may give evidence of the late first century situation of the stabilization of Old Greek translations; but most scriptural intertextuality in the NT gives clear evidence of the earlier period of textual fluidity similar to that in the Qumran literature.[9]

The other innovation of the *HUB* apparatus structure is its inclusion of readings from the Cairo Genizah.[10] With these two innovations, the history of the text is presented more fully than in any other critical edition of the Bible so far attempted. One should note, too, that both the Isaiah and the Jeremiah volumes have included readings from the

9   See J. A. Sanders, "The Dead Sea Scrolls and Biblical Studies" in *Sha'arei Talmon: Studies in the Bible, Qumran, and the Ancient Near East Presented to Shemaryahu Talmon*, M. Fishbane and E. Tov, eds., (Winona Lake: Eisenbrauns, 1992) pp. 326–29.

10   *BHQ* plans to include readings from the Cairo Genizah that date before 1000 CE. The *BHS* apparatus indiscriminately included some *genizah* readings.

newly recovered Firkowitch manuscripts in Russia, photographed and studied by Malachi Beit-Arié and others.[11] One does wonder, however, if the desire to present a full history of the text is to be realized if one can essentially overlook Origen's second column. Despite giving "pride of place" to the early versions in the first apparatus, the *HUB* shows a tendency to privilege the Hebrew language witnesses.

Most prior reviews of the Isaiah fascicles have highlighted the problem involved in grouping Judaean scrolls readings with rabbinic citations, but the editors are fully aware of the problem, and equally aware of the problems that would arise in constructing the apparatuses if they tried to set the historical shift from pre-masoretic to proto-masoretic at the beginning of the second century CE as the basic criterion, ignoring the distinction between text and versions.[12]

What is truly remarkable about the change that has taken place in the concept and theory of text criticism since the recovery of the Judaean Desert Scrolls and of Codex Aleppensis at the middle of this century is the importance of the classical Tiberian masora to understanding the text of the Hebrew Bible. It takes both *ketiv* and *qere* to make *Miqra!*[13]

11   See M. Beit-Arié, "The Accessibility of the Russian Manuscript Collections: New Perspectives for Jewish Studies," *The Folio: The Bulletin of the Ancient Biblical Manuscript Center for Preservation and Research* 13/1 (Winter 1995) pp. 1–7.

12   E.g., reviews of M. Goshen-Gottstein, *The Book of Isaiah, Sample Edition with the Introduction* (Jerusalem: The Hebrew University Bible Project, 1965) by P. A. H. de Boer in *JT* 16 (1966) pp. 247–52 and B. J. Roberts in *JTS* (1967) pp. 166–68. By contrast, see E. J. Revell's review of M. Goshen-Gottstein, ed., *The Book of Isaiah: Parts 1 and 2* (The Hebrew University Bible; Jerusalem: Magnes Press 1975) in *JBL* (1977) pp. 120–22.

13   See J. A. Sanders, "The Task of Text Criticism," in *Problems in Biblical Theology*, H. Sun, K. Eades, eds., (Grand Rapids: Eerdmans, 1997) pp. 315–27, esp. p. 316.

A quick glance at the history of modern, or post-Renaissance, text criticism will help. When, in 1519, Martin Luther translated the NT into German, he simply used Erasmus's text. But when, in 1523, he started work on translating the Hebrew Bible, he ran into text critical problems. He basically used the Brescia Bible of 1494 and often used the Vulgate to translate text-critically difficult texts. He devised a hermeneutic of text criticism in order to choose among variant readings. That hermeneutic, which he called *Res et Argumentum*, was very clear; one chose the reading that pointed forward to the gospel of Jesus Christ. (Of course, by that he meant his understanding of Paul's understanding of the gospel of Jesus Christ.) Following the lead of Elias Levita, Luther devalued the work of the masoretes, which meant one could vocalize and parse the consonantal text without the masoretic constraints of vowels, accents, and masorot. This gave license to several generations of scholars to emend the text almost at will, such as Capellus, Houbigant, Morin, Simon, and the whole Critica Sacra movement.

That situation led Baruch Spinoza in 1670 to publish his now famous tractate declaring that the truth of the Bible would be discovered in discerning the history of the formation of the biblical text and the authorial intentionality of its individual writers. In Spinoza, one saw the full result of the renaissance of Greek philosophy and culture which had begun in the fourteenth and fifteenth centuries: it was the original individual's thought that was inspired and authoritative. The community dimension of biblical literature, in which anonymity of authorship was common, succumbed to hellenization in many ways, including the pseudepigraphic attribution of biblical books to well-known community figures of the past. The Semitic perspective of community identity was considerably modified. Spinoza, in his genius, went on to say that such a history would probably never be complete, and discerning authorial intentionality would more than likely not be possible. Spinoza was declared *persona non grata* by both synagogue and church, but his influence, whether he was cited or not, was considerable.[14]

By the time of Johann David Michaelis in the eighteenth century, the hermeneutic had changed from having the aim of pointing to the gospel of Jesus Christ to reconstructing as far as possible the *ipssissima verba* of biblical authors, but the denigration of the work of the masoretes continued, since it clearly served the purpose of emending the text as exegesis of so-called original meanings indicated. In fact that aspect of Luther's hermeneutic persists in Old Testament scholarship today. Paul Kahle, whose work has probably been the most influential of any scholar in this century, dismissed the work of the masoretes as a creation of the Ben Asher family, in effect continuing to denigrate the oral traditions on which it drew.[15] *The Hebrew University Bible*, as well as *Biblia Hebraica Quinta*, in due course, will finally rectify that sad situation which has obtained since the sixteenth century. Both projects have, in effect, rehabilitated the worth and value of the work of the Tiberian masoretes for understanding the text of the Bible.[16] The corrective had begun with Gérard Weil's work on the masora for the *BHS*.

The HUBP struggled through a number of problems having to do with the logistics of constructing a critical text of the Bible. There were two precipices to avoid: on the one hand drowning the apparatus in innumerable alleged readings; or overworking the tools of analysis in order to pare

14   J. A. Sanders, "Hermeneutics of Text Criticism" esp. pp. 2–4.
15   P. Kahle, *Der hebräische Bibeltext seit Franz Delitzsch* (Stuttgart: Kohlhammer, 1961) p. 51. See the trenchant remarks by M. Goshen-Gottstein in "The Rise of the Tiberian Bible Text," in *Biblical and Other Studies*, ed. by Alexander Altmann (Cambridge: Harvard University Press, 1963) p. 89.
16   See the discussion by Barthélemy in *CTAT*, vol. 3 (1992) pp. ccxxviii-ccxxxviii.

down the number of notations.[17] The solution they arrived at is probably as circumspect as a critical edition of the Bible can be: to abandon eclectic apparatuses which quote supporting witnesses if exegesis requires it, but instead to construct five apparatuses, four of which would contain notations of the several types of variant witnesses; and a fifth which would offer the editors' subjective judgment as to which is a true variant. The four apparatuses offer first, the apparently variant readings in the ancient versions; the second, those in witnesses to the Hebrew text; the third, the medieval biblical manuscripts; and the fourth, masoretic variations in spelling, vowels, and accents. The editors contend that they have presented in those four apparatuses the basic history of the text *ad loc.*, and with very few exceptions they are very thorough indeed.[18]

It is the fifth/sixth apparatus, first in modern Hebrew and then the same in English, that offers the subjective judgments of the editors about the results of using text critical tools of analysis. This final apparatus hints at the eventual text critical commentary proposed for each volume. In many ways, the commentaries should provide the excitement which the fifth apparatus only teasingly suggests.[19]

HOTTP worked the other way round. Through Barthélemy's analytical reports in *CTAT*, we are providing in-depth text critical commentaries on over five thousand textual problems of all sorts. Those commentaries offer

17   As put by Goshen-Gottstein in *Text and Language in Bible and Qumran* (Jerusalem: Orient Publishing House, 1960) p. xiii.

18   Granting some of the points made by P. A. H. de Boer in his review of M. Goshen-Gottstein's *The Book of Isaiah* in *VT* 16, and the obvious observation that there is the subjectivity factor throughout the enterprise.

19   See the preliminary effort in S. Talmon—E. Tov, "A Commentary on the Text of Jeremiah 1. The LXX of Jeremiah 1:1–7," *Textus* 9 (1981) pp. 1–15.

extensive analyses of the history of the text for each problem addressed, from the earliest witnesses through the medieval grammarians and commentators, to the vagaries of modern critical research on the text. Now the work of constructing a handbook critical edition is in the hands of the next generation, the team working on *BHQ*.

The task of text criticism is to locate true variants, of whatever literary length, over against pseudo-variants. The aim of text criticism is to establish the date in the earliest history of transmission of the text when inner literary developments are basically complete and when ancient Jewish believing communities accepted those texts as functionally canonical (Talmon's *Gruppentexte*), at which text critical judgments are designed to point. The goal of text criticism is finally to provide the soundest possible base for establishing the critically most responsible text for reading and translation. And *HUB* and *BHQ* of necessity have as their major job to present the essential, critically considered history of the text for use by readers of any and all persuasions, no matter their aim.

A difficulty both projects have is one shared by all efforts to present a fully critical edition of the text, and that is caused by the constraints imposed by the goal sought, namely a printed, critical edition. Both projects have to apologize at the outset that the printed *mise-en-page* cannot reproduce precisely the manuscript used as base text. Instead of the three-column width page or folio of the manuscript, it is necessary for both to present the text in a single column. The masora magna has to be adjusted somewhat to make the printed page legible for scholars. And there are other adjustments demanded by the requirements of *mise-en-page*.

But considerably more important is the fact that due to the constraints of a printed critical edition, each text critical problem is presented in words and short phrases, leaving to the reader the all-important work of seeing those words and phrases in their fuller literary context. Time and again, we found on the HOTTP, and I assume this is the case for the teams producing both the *HUB* and *BHQ,* that it was not until we had placed the problem addressed in its fuller context that we could see what was really going on in the text and the place the problematic word or phrase had in that larger context. It is not until one can perceive the concept underlying the fuller text or version that one can understand why the variant text came to be. As Elias Bickerman pointed out, every translation was intended to serve the needs of the community for which it was translated.[20] This is sometimes the case even for copies of the Hebrew text itself, as with the large Isaiah Scroll, and most of the Qumran biblical texts. Every tradent, whether copyist or translator, had a concept of what the text he or she was handing on meant; and his or her concept of necessity was lodged in the cultural thought forms of the tradent and the community served.

Commonly, the concept we scholars attribute to a biblical text in its so-called original setting is not the one operative in the traditions derived from it. The later tradent may have had a cogent and consistent view of what the text meant in his or her contemporary cultural terms, and then slightly adapted the copy or translation at certain junctures in the text to fit that view. Fortunately, there are now available new subdisciplines of biblical study which can help us understand the underlying concept behind a text or translation, as well as better comprehend our own understanding of the text—specifically, structure and concept analysis.[21] The fuller text critical commentaries in *CTAT* well reflect the use of such analysis, but it is impossible, as far as I can see, to present the arguments of such

20   E. Bickerman, *Studies in Jewish and Christian History* (Leiden: Brill, 1976) vol. 2, p. 196.
21   See J. A. Sanders, "The Task of Text Criticism," in *Problems in Biblical Theology: Essays in Honor of Rolf Knierim,* H. Sun and K. Eades, eds., (Grand Rapids: Eerdmans, 1997) pp. 315–27, esp. pp. 326–27.

crucial studies in a printed critical edition of a text; only the bare results can be suggested, as they sometimes are indirectly in the fifth/sixth apparatus of the *HUB*. Text critical commentaries must reflect this aspect of the work of text criticism far more than they have to date in order to move the art of text criticism away from the tendency to think in terms of isolated words and short phrases.

This is perhaps not the place for me to present the case for the pluriform Bible, in which the larger contexts of variant understandings of the same text can be presented in full; but I feel compelled to mention it. This has begun to happen in Bibles that offer translations of the Hebrew Esther in the canonical Bible and translations of the Greek Esther, which presents quite a different concept of that wonderful story, in the so-called apocryphal section. And, of course, it also happens willy-nilly within the Hebrew Bible where there are doublets, such as the Ten Commandments, Psalm 18 / 2 Samuel 22, and many other doublets, even triplets. Full structure analysis of larger variant passages within biblical books will eventually, I think, show the necessity of presenting in parallel columns the Masoretic Text and the Septuagint understandings of the same story or pericope, simply because focus on the isolated words and short phrases does not present or even indicate the full history of the text.

Both the HUBP and the HOTTP fully realize that we have never before had an *editio critica maior* of the Hebrew Bible. The *Hebrew University Bible* may be as close to such that we will ever attain, and the fact that it does so permits *BHQ* essentially to remain a *Handausgabe* for more general use. The *HUB* places us pretty far down the road toward an *editio critica maior,* presenting a history of the text, book by book; and *CTAT* places us pretty far down the road toward what a text critical commentary should be, evaluating the whole history of textual problems addressed, book by book, from the earliest witnesses to the latest scholarly treatises.

The concept underlying both projects is based on the same understanding of the history of transmission of the text. They both agree that while exegesis will always be a limited part of the text critical enterprise, it cannot any longer be permitted to dominate it. And they both agree that the aim of text criticism can be neither to point to some future goal of history, nor to the primitive historical, even mythic origins of a text's authorial intentionality, nor even to the earliest stages of a text's transmission while it was still in literary development,[22] but to that point in its history when the text first became the common literature of a believing community.[23] And that point antedates both Christianity and Rabbinic Judaism.

If this is the case, then confessional differences among us should not be a stumbling block to producing a true *editio critica maior* together. *BHQ*, for the first time in the history of *Biblia Hebraica*, has Jews on the team preparing individual books.[24] The post-modern period provides the context in which to have true dialogue, not in this case about our differing confessional identities, but about the texts on which those identities are based. Because of the acerbic nature of the charges and counter-charges in the early centuries of Jewish/Christian debates about what the text was and what it meant, Origen provided a six-column comparison of the texts known to him in his time. He wanted the debate to become a dialogue.

---

22   *Pace* E. Tov in *Textual Criticism of the Hebrew Bible* (Minneapolis: Fortress, 1992) pp. 313–49.

23   See Talmon's remarks in "The Textual Study of the Bible—A New Outlook," in *Qumran and the History of the Biblical Text* (Cambridge: Harvard University Press, 1975) p. 325, in which he rejects the "three local texts" hypothesis in favor of understanding some texts as accepted by "a sociologically definable integrated body," in our terms, a believing community, hence rendering that accepted text functionally canonical for that community.

24   David Marcus (Ezra-Nehemiah), Leonard Greenspoon (Joshua), Abraham Tal (Genesis), and Zipporah Talshir (1–2 Chronicles).

All of us in this room, Jew, Christian, and secular, are to some extent or another children of the Renaissance in Europe of Greco-Roman culture, or we would not participate in such a conference as this. And now we are moving into a period of intellectual history in which we are forced to realize that the observer is a part of the observed, and objectivity is but subjectivity under constraint. What better constraint can there be than dialogue in which our own most precious premises are carefully and thoughtfully critiqued by those who stand elsewhere? As Ferdinand Deist aptly put it, critique should not have the purpose of destroying the other's position, but to correct and strengthen it for the sake of true dialogue at a yet higher level.[25]

Just as both projects agree that textual analysis should lead to the location of true variants, that is, to a point where the arguments on both sides of a potential textual variant are equally strong so that neither can be eliminated, thereby indicating the existence of a true variant,[26] so we should now move beyond competition to see who is right, to co-operation to see what is right for the sake of all the communities we serve, whether confessional or professional. The day when the idea that individual schools or individual scholars alone can arrive at the truth of a text, and all others would eventually see the light, is gone.

There is no question that the ASOR has made crucial contributions over these fifty years to understanding the history of the transmission of the text of the Hebrew Bible through the work of its members and friends on the Judaean Desert Scrolls.

---

25 F. Deist, *Witnesses to the Old Testament* (Pretoria: NG Kerkboekhandel, 1988) pp. 160–63. (The writer received the sad news that Deist died in Heidelberg, on leave from Stellenbosch, on July 12.)

26 Well expressed by Goshen-Gottstein in *Text and Language* p. 201.

Was Qumran, Indeed, a Monastery?
The Consensus and Its Challengers, an Archaeologist's View

Magen Broshi

On February 6, 1948, E. L. Sukenik wrote in his diary: ". . . I think that the *genizah* belongs to the Essenes."[1] This was just two months after Sukenik had identified the scrolls as Second Commonwealth manuscripts. He published his theory in the summer of the same year,[2] and it soon gained a status of near consensus.

1   Y. Yadin, "A Biography of E. L. Sukenik," *Eretz Israel* 8 (1967) p. 18 [in Hebrew]. The term *genizah* denotes a cache of unusable manuscripts written in Hebrew characters. As will be learned later that the scrolls were not put in the caves because of their unusability. However, the root *gnz* was made a component in the Hebrew name of the Dead Sea Scrolls.

2   E. L. Sukenik, *Hidden Scrolls, First Report* (Jerusalem: Bialik, 1948) p.16 [in Hebrew]. It is interesting to note that this slim, elegant volume was printed during the War of Independence, while Jerusalem was under heavy shelling.

However, in short time the consensus camp was surrounded by quite a big number of vociferous dissenters raising all kinds of claims—from allegation that the scrolls are modern forgeries to all possible and impossible identifications, practically with every conceivable candidate in Judaism and early Christianity. This will be the topic of the second part of this paper, in which we will try to describe and explain the proliferation of the dissent, its vitality after half a century of polemics, and some of the characteristics of the anti-consensual theories. We shall mention here one typical feature: all those theories are hardly ever held by more than one person, their progenitors. In the following we shall try to assess the archaeological aspect of the Essene theory, i.e., was Qumran indeed an Essene monastery? For this purpose we will call upon seven witnesses to testify. First to enter the witness stand will be an important Roman author, a contemporary of the last residents of Qumran.

Pliny the Elder probably had never been to Qumran, but there is no reason to doubt the reliability of his testimony. In his *Historia Naturalis* (V,73) he says that:

> On the west side of the Dead Sea, but out of the range of the noxious exhaltations of the coast, is the solitary tribe of the Essenes . . . it has no women and has renounced all sexual desire, has no money and has only palm trees for company . . ." (trans. H. Rackham, Loeb Classical Library).

The reason why Pliny does not use the term monastery is because the Latin vocabulary of his time did not yet possess this word—the Essene establishment was the first of its kind in the western world. Pliny ends his passage on the Essenes by saying that below them (*infra hos*) was formerly the town of Engeda (i.e., Ein Gedi). Much ink has been spilled over the interpretation of the expression "below them," but it seems pretty certain that Pliny who proceeds in his description from north to south, as if the direction is downstream, should regard the southern locality to be below the northern one.[3] The western shore of the Dead Sea has been surveyed literally scores of times. Qumran is the only site that suits Pliny's data. As we shall see later, the archaeological finds at Qumran agree very well with what we ought to expect.

The contemporary historians Philo and Josephus do not mention that the Essenes are connected to the Dead Sea,[4] but they tell us that they led a celibate way of life. Pliny and Philo (*Hypothetica* 11,14) speak only about their abstention from marriage, but Josephus, who is well aware of their negative attitude to matrimony (*War* 2,120), knows also of Essenes who lead more or less normal familial life (*War* 2,160). However, three historians, two Jewish (Philo, Josephus) and one pagan (Pliny) speak about their celibate contingent and Qumran is the likeliest site for their center.

The Dead Sea Scrolls can testify that Qumran was inhabited by celibate Essenes. First, it is impossible to separate between the scrolls and the Qumran compound as was suggested by some scholars.[5] The same distinctive pottery jars are found in the Community Center as in the caves.[6] To some of the caves, like Cave 7, one could enter only through the compound and others, like Cave 4, where three-fourths of the manuscripts were found, are so close to the compound that it is inconceivable that anybody outside the community was allowed to use them. In short, the caves, especially the artificial ones that were dug in the marl

3   J. P. Audet, "Qumran et la notice de Pline sur les Essenienne," *RQ* 68 (1961) pp. 364–87 and M. Stern, *Greek and Latin Authors on Jews and Judaism*, vol. 1, (Jerusalem: The Israel Academy, 1974) pp. 472, 480–81.

4   This was done only by Pliny and Dio Chrisostom. Cf. M. Stern, *Greek and Latin Authors on Jews and Judaism*, vol. 1, pp. 538–40.

5   E.g., N. Golb, *Who Wrote the Dead Sea Scrolls?: The Search for the Secret of Qumran* (New York: Scribner, 1995).

6   R. de Vaux, *Archaeology and the Dead Sea Scrolls* (Oxford: Oxford University Press, 1973).

terrace, cannot be separated from the compound. Second, the "library" of Qumran[7] has an unmistakable Essene character and it cannot be described as a haphazard medley of Jewish books. Indeed, the "sectarian" books, while constituting a sizable part of the books, do not play an exclusive role.[8] What is of utmost significance is that this large literary body has only books of religious nature and almost nothing that can be ascribed to the opponents of the Essenes, the Pharisees and the Sadducees. The backbone of this "library" is sectarian, as most scholars agree, Essene books. These are the books which appear in many copies—like the *Rule of the Community* of which we have eleven exemplars,

7   The scrolls found at Qumran do not constitute a library in a strict sense—libraries did not exist in Jewish Palestine of the Second Commonwealth. See Y. Shavit, "The 'Qumran Library' in the Light of the Attitude towards Books in the Second Temple Period," in *Methods of Investigation of the Dead Sea Scrolls and the Khirbet Qumran Site: Present Realities and Future Prospects*, Michael O. Wise, et al., eds., Annals of the New York Academy of Sciences (New York: New York Academy of Sciences, 1994) pp. 299–317 and M. Haran, "Bible Scrolls in Eastern and Western Communities from Qumran to the High Middle Ages," *HUCA* 56 (1985) pp. 21–62. Jewish libraries came into existence only about a millennium after the demise of Qumran.

8   D. Dimant, "The Qumran Manuscripts: Contents and Significance" in *Time to Prepare the Way in the Wilderness* D. Dimant and L. Schiffman, eds., (Leiden: Brill, 1995) pp. 23–58, whose criteria are topical and linguistic, and E. Tov, "The Orthography and Language of the Hebrew Scrolls found at Qumran and the Origin of these Scrolls," *Textus* 13 (1986) pp. 32–57 and "Scribal Practices Reflected in the Documents from the Judean Desert and in the Rabbinic Literature: A Comparative Study," in M. Fox, et al., eds., Texts, Temples, and Traditions: A Tribute to Menachem Haran (Winnona Lake: Eisenbrauns, 1996) pp. 383–403, whose criteria are the peculiarities of the Qumran scribal school: orthography, morphology, etc.

The *Damascus Document* preserved in ten copies etc. More-over, even compositions which are not Qumranic *senso strictu*, but show great kinship, are very popular. From *Jubi-lees*, a book which has much in common with the Qumran-ites—foremost the calendar (not a trifle)—there are fifteen copies. This certainly is not the place to explain in detail why the scrolls have been ascribed to the Essenes, but we would like to underline the amazing similarity between what Josephus tells about the Essenes and what the sectar-ian scrolls tell about their authors. It runs the whole gamut from the trivial, e.g., the prohibition on spitting while sit-ting in a midst of a group ("The man who spits into the midst of the assembly of the Many shall be punished for thirty days," *Rule of the Community* 7.3; cf. *Jewish War* 2.147) to their belief in predestination (in particular *Rule of the Community* 3:13 – 4:26; *Antiquities* 18.18–22), which was undoubtedly the most important single element in their theology.[9]

That the Essene movement included both celibate members and "family men" can be gathered also from the scrolls. In the *Rule of the Community*, no women and children are mentioned, a most significant omission as women are quite problematic creatures, a source of impurity. One can compare the stringent rules concerning women in the *Temple Scroll*—no sexual activity is to take place within the confines of the Temple City.[10] Women and children are barred from the camps in the *War Scroll*, perhaps because of their seductive properties.[11] There were also marrying

9   E. H. Merrill, *Qumran and Predestination: A Theological Study of the Thanksgiving Hymns* (Leiden: E. J. Brill, 1975) and T. S. Beall, *Josephus' Description of the Essenes Illustrated by the Dead Sea Scrolls* (Cambridge: Cambridge University Press, 1988).

10   Y. Yadin, *The Temple Scroll*, 3 vols., (Jerusalem: Israel Exploration Society, 1983).

11   Y. Yadin, *The Scroll of the War of the Sons of Light against the Sons of Darkness* (Oxford: Oxford University Press, 1962).

Essenes. "And if they live in camps . . . marrying and begetting children" (*Damascus Document* 7:6–9). *The Rule of the Congregation* speaks about women and children (1QSa 1:4–5) and that a man "shall not [approach] a woman to know her by lying with her before he is fully twenty years old" (1QSa 1:9–10). There is hardly a doubt that the Qumran Essenes were the celibate ones.

The first three witnesses were literary. Now we will call to the stand four archaeological witnesses.

The Immersion Pools (*Miqwaot*)

The existence of ten such pools in an area no larger than one acre is the strongest argument for defining Qumran as a religious site. Nowhere in Palestine, where three hundred *miqwaot* have been unearthed, do we have such big pools or such density of these religious installations. These cisterns have distinct features in which one cannot err: staircases with symbolic partition walls meant to demarcate the division between the descending impure and the ascending pure.[12] The concern for ritual bathing was common to all religious parties in Second Commonwealth Palestine, but nowhere can one see such a rabid concern.

Potter's Workshop

This is prima facie an indifferent installation, indeed an indicator that the inhabitants of Qumran were very keen on matters of ritual purity.[13] There was no economic justification for keeping a potter's atelier and two kilns for a

12　R. Reich, "The Bath House (Balneum), the Miqweh and the Jewish Community in the Second Temple Period," *JJS* 39 (1988) pp. 102–7, and M. Broshi and H. Eshel, "How and Where Did the Qumranites Live?," in *Proceedings of the 1996 International Conference on the Dead Sea Scrolls*, D. W. Parry and E. Ulrich, eds., (Leiden: Brill, forthcoming).

13　M. Goodman, "A Note on Qumran Sectarians, the Essenes and Josephus," *JJS* 46 (1995) pp. 161–66.

century or a century and a half to serve a small and austere community in a site which does not enjoy the benefits of cheap energy or good clay.[14] The nature of Qumran pottery testifies not only to austerity,[15] but also to the insistence on self reliance and the production of vessels on which purity no doubt can be cast. It could very well be that Qumran might have supplied its ware to other Essene communities.[16]

The Common Dining Room

The common dining room, as well as the kitchen, pantry, flour mill, etc., show that the people who lived here led a communal mode of life.[17] A comparison with Masada of the Sicarii, almost a contemporary, is quite instructive. Here, a household mode of life was led. The site, especially in the wall casemates, is replete with stoves, baking ovens, silos, and the like.[18]

The Necropolis

Of all the components of the Qumran complex, the cemetery (or rather cemeteries) is the most discussed in scholarship, and for obvious reasons.[19] The vast

14   R. de Vaux, *Archaeology and the Dead Sea Scrolls*, pp. 4, 6, 7, 16–17; J. B. Humbert and A. Chambon, *Fouilles de Khirbet Qumran et de Ain Feshkha* (Fribourg: Editions universitaires; Göttingen: Vandenhoeck & Ruprecht, 1994). See loci 64, 70, 75, and 84.

15   J. Magness, "A Villa at Khirbet Qumran?," *RQ* 63 (1994) pp. 397–419.

16   M. Broshi and H. Eshel, "How and Where Did the Qumranites Live?," forthcoming.

17   R. de Vaux, *Archaeology and the Dead Sea Scrolls*.

18   E. Netzer, *Masada 3: The Buildings, Stratigraphy, and Architecture* (Jerusalem: Israel Exploration Society, 1991) pp. 461ff.

19   R. de Vaux, *Archaeology and the Dead Sea Scrolls*, pp. 45–48, 57–58; S. Steckroll, "The Community of the Dead Sea Scrolls," in *Centro Studi e Documentatzione sull' Italia Romana*

necropolis comprises twelve hundred graves of a completely new type: shaft graves, up to two meters deep, in which the deceased lie supine facing north. Since the excavations of Qumran, a few small, similar cemeteries were found, mostly near the northwestern shore of the Dead Sea and one, with some fifty burials, near Jerusalem.[20]

The necropolis is made of a central cemetery with some eleven hundred graves and subsidiary extensions with one hundred graves. In the central graveyard, where the tombs are arranged in straight lines, only male skeletons were unearthed; in the "extensions," where the tombs are in disarray, were found also nine skeletons of women and six of children. Thus, women and children constitute some 30 percent of the burials (fifteen out of fifty-two). In pre-industrial societies women and children make up some 70 percent of the population.

In five of the tombs, remains of wooden coffins were found. This most probably shows that bodies were brought from a considerable distance. In three graves, the skeletons were found disjointed, with some parts missing. This indicates that we have here cases of secondary burials and that these remains were also brought from some other place. Thus, it seems that the central graveyard, where only male

V (Milano: Cisalpino-Goliardica, 1973–74) pp. 199–244; M. Broshi, "The Archaeology of Qumran—A Reconsideration," in *The Dead Sea Scrolls: Forty Years of Research*, D. Dimant and U. Rappaport, eds., (Leiden/Jerusalem: Brill/Magnes, 1992) pp. 103–15; J. B. Humbert and A. Chambon, *Fouilles de Khirbet Qumran et de Ain Feshkha*, pp. 213–27, 346–52; M. Broshi and H. Eshel, *How and Where Did the Qumranites Live?*, forthcoming.

20   B. Zissu, "Field Graves at Beit Zafafa: Archaeological Evidence for the Essene Community," in *New Studies on Jerusalem: Proceedings of the Second Conference* (Ramat Gan: Bar Ilan University, 1996) pp. 32–40; I. A. Baumgarten, "The Temple Scroll, Toilet Practices, and the Essenes," *Jewish History* 10 (1996) pp. 9–20.

skeletons were found, was reserved for the members of the Qumran community and that in the fringe were buried relatives, germane or spiritual. In short, there is no doubt that the burials do not represent only members of the Community and that the existence of women and children should not be used as a proof that the Qumran Community was not celibate.[21]

The mode of burial at Qumran is very much what one would expect: a total break with the traditional Jewish customs.[22] The Qumran burials are individual, unlike the family burials practiced in Judaism from time immemorial. The Essene insistence that their members should sever their ties with their families is hinted at by Josephus ("But it is not permitted to give gifts to relatives without the consent of the stewards," *War* 2.134) as well as in the scrolls: a member of the Community is rebuked for his misdemeanor of "loving his kinsman."[23]

I hope that the seven witnesses—three literary and four archaeological—have been sufficient to convince all that Qumran was indeed a monastery.

The non-consensual theories (and we shall deal only with those which refer only to the archaeological aspects of Qumran) suggest that this site was a farm (or rather a villa rustica), a fortress, or a caravanserai. Other theories which have been brought to our notice, viz., that the site was a leper house or a plant for producing papyrus will not be discussed here as they haven't yet appeared in press. The first test of these theories should be their ability to answer

21   L. H. Schiffman, *Reclaiming the Dead Sea Scrolls* (Philadelphia and Jerusalem: Jewish Publication Society, 1994) p. 129.
22   R. Hachlili, "Burial Practices at Qumran," *RQ* 16 (1993) pp. 247–64.
23   E. Eshel, "4Q477: 'The Rebukes by the Overseer'," *JJS* 45 (1994) pp. 111–22; I. A. Baumgarten, The Temple Scroll, Toilet Practices and the Essenes, *Jewish History* 10 (1996) pp. 17–18, n. 18.

adequately a series of questions: why should a villa rustica (or a fortress, or a caravanserai, etc.) have no less than ten immense immersion pools? What is a cemetery of twelve hundred burials doing there? What are the scrolls doing in such a place? How is it that a caravanserai does not have big enough living quarters (or for that matter a villa rustica) for the masters or the staff? If there was a second story dormitory in Qumran, it could not have accommodated more than a dozen inmates.[24] If any of these theories is right, where is the Essene settlement Pliny tells us about? I am afraid that the authors of these theories have not offered us any satisfactory answers to these questions, but let us examine these theories per se.

It ought to be reiterated that few areas in the world have been investigated as thoroughly as the shores of the Dead Sea and Qumran is the only candidate to the site described by Pliny.

A Villa Rustica?

R. Donceel and P. Donceel-Voûte propose that the site served as a rustic villa. In addition to the questions posed above, one is entitled to ask why should anyone bother to establish a villa here. There is no agricultural potential in this barren site. Its marly, salty soil does not grow even scant weeds in winter, and the palm grove which must have existed at nearby Ein Feshkha does not need permanent care—the architectural remains found there testify to constructions which could have served the seasonal tenders of this grove. Unlike the elegant palaces and villas of Jericho, which enjoyed an excellent supply of good water, Qumran had to rely on flash flood water which must have spoiled after a few months of exposure in the intensive heat of the Rift Valley or the brackish water of Ein Feshkha.

---

24   M. Broshi and H. Eshel, *How and Where Did the Qumranites Live?*, forthcoming.

Jodi Magness has shown in great detail that jerry-built Qumran has none of the features we should expect from a Second Commonwealth villa rustica.[25] "The most compelling argument against the identification of Qumran as a villa lies in the almost complete absence of interior decoration."[26] P. Donceel-Voûte's most important argument is that the room above locus 30, which was identified (it seems, justifiably) by de Vaux as a scriptorium is in fact a cenacle, i.e., a dining room, or by another name a triclinium.[27] She is of the opinion that the "tables" found there are nothing but *klinai*, i.e., couches. This suggestion should be rejected on plain technical grounds: the couches, tapering with a curve towards the floor are not sturdy enough to carry the weight of an adult diner. Moreover, they are very narrow for *klinai* and Donceel-Voûte herself admits that she cannot quote any parallels for such couches, neither in artistic representations nor archaeological finds.[28]

A Fortress?

In a series of lengthy articles, and lately in a book, N. Golb, has offered an elaborate counter-paradigm intended to replace the consensual one.[29] We shall discuss here only his

25 J. Magness, "A Villa at Khirbet Qumran?," *RQ* 63 (1994) pp. 397–419.
26 J. Magness, "A Villa at Khirbet Qumran?," p. 412
27 P. Donceel-Voûte, "'Coenaculum': La salle à l'étage du locus 30 à Khirbet Qumran sur la Mer Morte" in *Banquets d'Orient* (Res Orientales IV; Leuven: Peeters, 1992) pp. 61–84.
28 P. Donceel-Voûte, "'Coenaculum': La salle à l'étage du locus 30 à Khirbet Qumran sur la Mer Morte" passim; R. Reich, "A Note on the Function of Room 30 (the 'Scriptorium') at Khirbet Qumran," *JJS* 46 (1996) pp. 157–60.
29 N. Golb, *Who Wrote the Dead Sea Scrolls?* (New York: Scribner, 1995).

points which have archaeological aspects.[30] First, we
address his claim that Qumran was not an Essene monastery, but a link in a ring of fortresses which defended Jerusalem, Masada being another of these forts. Needless to
say, the comparison of Masada and Qumran is somewhat
far-fetched. Qumran is not a fortress at all. Its walls, which
are made of ill fitting undressed stones, are quite flimsy.
Their width (60–70 cm.) does not suit a fortified compound, and its unguarded entrances cannot belong to a
military structure. The site lies in an isolated, strategically
worthless point. The north-south road passing nearby did
not exist until a few years ago. Its course was blocked by the
cliffs jutting into the Dead Sea just south of Ein Feshkha.
Only the receding of the sea, a phenomenon which started
recently due to the use of the waters of the rivers Jordan
and Yarmuk by Israel and Jordan, allowed the construction
of a road along the shore. All through history, traffic passed
west of the cliffs, above Qumran, and over which Qumran
had no control.

The second point raised by Golb is that no manuscripts
were found in the compound. As a matter of fact, the
chances of manuscripts surviving the fire set by the con-
querors of the site, probably in June 68 CE, were very slim.
Even slimmer were the chances once the site was occupied
by a Roman garrison (Qumran Period 3).

The third point we would like to tackle is Golb's explanation of the cemetery as the place in which the Jewish
defenders of the alleged "fortress" were buried. A quick
glance can show even to the non-expert that in Qumran
there is no standing room for twelve hundred people, not
even for a small fraction of this number. It is hard to imagine that the Roman army bothered to bury twelve hundred

30   Cf. F. García Martínez and A. van der Woude, "A 'Grön-
     igen' Hypothesis of Qumran Origins and Early History,"
     RQ 14 (1990) pp. 526–36.

corpses in graves up to two meters deep. If a victorious army chooses to bury the dead of the vanquished—if only for hygienic purposes—it will do it only in shallow mass graves. It is not just crass inhumanity (which is the rule of battles), but there is also an urgent time factor. The corpses have to be buried quickly before they rot.[31]

A Caravanserai?

It was recently suggested that Qumran was an inn made to serve caravans going to Jerusalem.[32] This suggestion lacks topographical logic—no roads, major or otherwise, pass by Qumran. A likely place for a caravanserai would have been at the mouth of the Qedron dry riverbed, along which an important road leads to the capital, and where the Hasmoneans built a fortress, called in Arabic justly Qasr el-Yahud.[33] If Qumran indeed served caravans that crossed the sea by boats (camels loaded on boats is a most unlikely possibility, never recorded in the history of the Dead Sea), then one should expect a quay on the shore, like the

31 Z. J. Kapera, in his "Some Remarks on the Qumran Cemetery" in *Methods of Investigation of the Dead Sea Scrolls and the Khirbet Qumran Site: Present Realities and Future Prospects*, Michael O. Wise, et al., eds., pp. 97–113, vacillates between the accepted wisdom and Golb's theory, and comes up with the least satisfactory solution: both are right. To prove his point that the cemetery was used for the burial of war casualties, he quotes the study of N. Haas and H. Nathan, "Anthropological Survey on the Human Skeletal Remains from Qumran," *RQ* (1967–69) pp. 345–52, where they discuss a fractured skull. What he failed to see is that the fracture has been long healed and that the wounded man lived long after the incidence.

32 A. Crown, "Qumran—Was it an Essene Settlement?," *BARev* 20:5 (1994) pp. 24–36, 73–78.

33 P. Bar Adon, *Excavations in the Judaean Desert Atiqot* 9 [Hebrew Series] (Jerusalem: Israel Antiquities Authority, 1989) pp. 18–29.

one found on the opposite shore at Ain ez-Zara,[34] but no installation like this was found in the vicinity of Qumran. The Qumran compound lacks any of the components one should expect in a caravanserai, for instance, large stables or fireplaces for the wayfarers to cook their own meals. One could find many more arguments to discredit the three theories mentioned above, but we are convinced that those adduced here are sufficient to prove the principal weaknesses of these theories.

The Qumran Paradox

We have mentioned three archaeological theories, but they are only a small part of the non-consensual theories, of which we have no less than a dozen. This is not as bad as in the case of the *Damascus Document*, the first Dead Sea Scroll, which was found in the Cairo *genizah* exactly half a century before the discovery of the Qumran Scrolls. This well preserved invaluable book was ascribed by seventeen scholars to as many candidates.[35] But it should be remembered that the turn-of-the-century scholars did not have at their disposal the vast corpus we have today—100,000 words, not counting the biblical scrolls, detailed and well informed testimonies of their contemporaries Philo, Josephus, and Pliny and a wealth of archaeological data gained at the excavations of Qumran. It is beyond the scope of this paper to explain the paradoxical proliferation of ill founded theories. Let us just suggest three reasons:

1. The discovery of the scrolls, a truly serendipitous event, was so unexpected and so revolutionary that it

---

34   H. Schult, "Zwei Häfen aus römisher Zeit am Totem Meer," *ZDPV* 82 (1966) pp. 139–48; A. Clamer, "Ain ez-Zara Excavations," *Annual of the Department of Antiquities of Jordan* 33 (1989) pp. 217–25.
35   S. Ivry, "Was There a Migration to Damascus? The Problem of *by y*l*," *Eretz Israel* 9 (1969) pp. 80–88.

constituted a trauma to some of the first generation of scholars. For some of the venerable students of the Second Commonwealth, the introduction of the new finds was a violent invasion that interfered with their established world-image. Being in a state of shock, certain scholars offered strange ideas, such as claiming that the scrolls are modern forgeries.

2. The game has been played with no clear set of rules, therefore it attracted a lot of unqualified players. People whose expertise (in many cases considerable) lay in other fields, felt free to take part and issue ill founded opinions. For instance, some of the prominent non-consensual scholars do not have sufficient command of Hebrew and none of Aramaic. Were they physicians, their licenses would have been long ago revoked.

3. For the past half century, the Dead Sea Scrolls were in the limelight, not only because they are among the most important archaeological discoveries of our century, and not only being contemporary with Jesus but also, to a large degree, because of the scandals which followed from the outset. Was it true that the Vatican and the State of Israel were in cahoots not to publish the scrolls? Regrettably, much of the scrolls' fame (and notoriety too) are a *succes de scandal*. Are there grounds to the rumor that the scrolls contain embarrassing material and that Catholic scholars try to conceal such passages? It is a sad fact that university professors spread such shameful allegations. The Dead Sea Scrolls scholarship suffered from the fact it afforded its students, especially its mavericks, an opportunity to see their names in the *New York Times* and other prestigious dailies. One could do honest, serious work, all one's life and not be honored by the press outside the campus. Quite a number of scholars could not resist the temptation, as long as their names were spelled properly, preferably on the front page.

Undoubtedly, no branch of scholarship has been plagued by so many bogus problems. Why do Philo and Josephus not agree in all details? (Answer: Josephus had his information firsthand, Philo did not. Philo had also an idealizing tendency.) How come there are discrepancies between the *Damascus Document* and the *Rule of the Community*? (Answer: The former is concerned with non-celibate Essenes, the latter with the monastic Community.) Why are the Essenes described by Josephus differ from the Qumranites in their hygienic practices? (Answer: The differences are due to the difference between rural areas [where one had to use a mattock, as prescribed in the Pentateuch] and urban areas [where one had to use latrines—in rocky, crowded Jerusalem, mattocks would not be of much help]). We believe our answers are correct and adequate and, had they been heeded by scholars, much ink would have been spared.

It should be remembered that discrepancies are the rule in human reports, not the exception. Try to compare what various people, say, for example, about Paris. Often, it will seem as if they speak about different cities altogether. All the more so when it comes to different compositions, written for different purposes to different audiences. Remembering that ought to save a lot of quibbling.

The Scrolls and Robert McNamara

In my sophomore year in the Hebrew University, almost half a century ago, a brilliant young lecturer, a medievalist, asked me: "How could one rely on Albright (at that time, the esteemed mentor of archaeology) who keeps saying all the time that he now admits being wrong on this or that point?" My answer then, as it would be today, was that this is exactly the sign of his greatness, the ability to revise one's work, to correct one's own mistakes and admit in public to his change of mind.

Yet, admitting to being wrong means a certain loss of face, and, when coupled with human inflexibility, not many scholars would publicly declare that they have taken a wrong stand. Still, it is not altogether a rare phenomenon. In archaeology, my chosen field, I can think of two outstanding examples: Nelson Glueck and Glyn Daniel. Glueck, an innovative pioneer of Palestinian archaeology, devoted most of his career to surveys in Transjordan and the Negev. However, the most important biblical site which he excavated was arguably Tell Khleifeh, between Eilat and Aqabah. Glueck believed the place to be the biblical Ezion-Geber, and in its remains he saw signs of an important metallurgical center. A couple of decades later, when it was pointed out by other scholars that the site is no more than a fortress, he publicly endorsed the new interpretation.[36] Our second example has to do with Daniel, a British archaeologist who wrote his doctoral thesis on European megaliths and devoted a great deal of his career to these fascinating constructions. Nevertheless, after many years of publishing and teaching his theories, he concluded that he was wrong about the dates of those edifices, as well as about their origin. "It was the radiocarbon revolution, the greatest breakthrough in the history of archaeology, that brought us to our senses."[37]

In Dead Sea Scrolls scholarship, there are no cases like these, not even after the publication of new material or the revolutionary results of two rounds of radiocarbon 14 tests, results which prove definitely that the various "Christian" theories (and there are several) are chronologically impossible.[38] There were cases of admitting to minor, technical

36 N. Gleuck, "Ezion Geber," *BA* 28 (1965) pp. 20–87.
37 G. Daniel, *Some Small Harvest* (London: Thames and Hudson, 1986).
38 M. Broshi, "The New Radiocarbon Dates of the Dead Sea Scrolls and their Significance" in *The Practical Impact of Science on Near Eastern and Agean Archaeology*, S. H. Pike and S. Gitin, eds., *The Practical Impact of Science on Field Archaeology*, vol. 2, The Wiener Laboratories Publications III, (London: The Wiener Laboratories, 1998) forthcoming.

mistakes, such as the theatrical declaration of de Vaux thrice uttered: "je me suis trompe."[39]

In short, there were cases in which scholars admitted mistakes, usually *sotto voce*, but never errors. In fifty years and after about twelve thousand scholarly publications,[40] we do not find even one case of a scholar having the moral courage, decency, or intelligence—not to speak of all three—to stand up and say: "I have been wrong."

What a contrast to the noble public confession of Robert McNamara, who admitted his responsibility for the death and mutilation of hundreds of thousands of people. In his memoir, the secretary of defense during the Vietnam War (1961–1968), in which 58,000 American soldiers lost their lives and many more Vietnamese perished, he showed the moral bravery of admitting to an error immeasurably greater than authoring a wrong theory.

Conclusion

I cannot think of a more apt way to conclude this paper than by quoting the wise words of one the founders of the Dead Sea Scrolls research and one of its revered mentors, F. M. Cross:

> The scholar who would "exercise caution" in iden-
> tifying the sect of Qumran with Essenes places himself
> in an astonishing position: he must suggest seriously
> that two major parties formed communistic religious

---

39 In this case, about the dating and nature of the scrolls' pottery. Cf. R. de Vaux, "Suite aux manuscrits de la Mer Morte," *CRAIBL,* 1952, pp. 173–80.

40 A rough computation based on C. Burchard, *Bibliography zu Handschriften von Toten Meer,* 2 vols., (Berlin: Alfred Toeplmann, 1957, 1965), B. Jongeling, *A Classified Bibliography of the Finds in the Desert of Judah: 1958–1969* (Leiden: Brill, 1971) and F. García Martínez and D. W. Parry, *A Bibliography of the Finds in the Desert of Judah: 1970–95* (Leiden: Brill, 1996).

communities in the same district of the desert of the
Dead Sea and lived together in effect for two centuries,
holding similar bizarre views, performing similar or
rather identical lustrations, religious meals, and cere-
monies. He must suppose that one, carefully described
by classical authors, disappeared without leaving building remains or even potsherds behind; the other, sys-
tematically ignored by classical sources, left extensive
ruins, and indeed a great library. I prefer to be reckless
and flatly identify the men from Qumran with their
perennial houseguests, the Essenes.[41]

If they were Essenes, then something seems to be quite
clear: Qumran was a monastery.

41   F. M. Cross, "The Early History of the Qumran Commu-
     nity," in D. N. Freedman and J. C. Greenfield, eds., *New
     Directions in Biblical Archaeology* (New York: Doubleday,
     1969) pp. 68–69.

How Archaeology Affects the Study of Texts

Reflections on the Category "Rewritten Bible" at Qumran

Sidnie White Crawford

In recent years, as scholars have begun the long overdue reinvestigation of the archaeology of Khirbet Qumran, the complaint has often been heard that the existence of the texts from the eleven caves surrounding the site of Qumran has affected the archaeological interpretation of the ruins. Would Roland de Vaux, the excavator of Qumran, have identified the ruins as a communal settlement of a particular group of Jews, the Essenes, if he had not been aware of the contents of the scrolls, especially documents such as the *Rule of the Community*? The question is rhetorical; the answer, of course, is no. Thus, Pauline Donceel-Voûte can say, "with the finding of the scrolls, Qumran archaeology just seems to have stopped."[1] I am happy to

---

1   P. Donceel-Voûte, "The Archaeology of Khirbet Qumran," in *Methods of Investigation of the Dead Sea Scrolls and the Khirbet Qumran Site: Present Realities and Future Prospects*, M. O. Wise, N. Golb, J. Collins and D. Pardee, eds., (New York: New York Academy of Sciences, 1994) p. 34.

report that this is no longer true and that there have been many exciting and thought-provoking studies of Qumran archaeology recently, illustrated by the popularity of the archaeology sections at the Jerusalem Dead Sea Scrolls Congress in July, 1997.[2]

However, I would like to approach the relationship of archaeology and texts from a slightly different angle. While the discovery of the texts may have affected the interpretation of the archaeology, it is equally true that the archaeology affected the interpretation of the texts. That is, once de Vaux had identified Qumran as an Essene settlement, and especially once he had identified one of the loci (locus 30) as a "scriptorium" where scrolls were copied, the scrolls were identified as an Essene library.[3] This influenced our understanding of the texts in this way: if the library was the collection of a particular sect, living in isolation in the desert, then the texts were not representative of a wider Judaism of the period. Now, this reasoning did not have much impact on the biblical texts, or even the previously known apocryphal and pseudepigraphical texts, which were obviously known and preserved outside of Qumran. It is the previously unknown non-biblical texts that were most heavily affected by this reasoning. They were unknown prior to the discovery of the scrolls and they were found in the eleven caves associated with Qumran; hence they must be Essene compositions, copied or even composed at Qumran. Thus, they were scrutinized for what they might say about Essenes, but not about Judaism in general (as if the two were completely separate!). So Frank Moore Cross

2   See the forthcoming volume, *The Dead Sea Scrolls—Fifty Years After Their Discovery: Proceedings of the Jerusalem Congress, July 10–25, 1997*, L. H. Schiffman, E. Tov and J. VanderKam, eds., (Jerusalem: Israel Exploration Society, forthcoming).

3   R. de Vaux, *Archaeology and the Dead Sea Scrolls* (London: Oxford University Press, 1973), especially the section entitled "The Ruins and the Texts."

could say "in [the Cave 4] texts we find a cross section of the literature of *sectarian* Judaism at the end of the pre-Christian era."[4] Now, however, few scholars would accept that statement. The present consensus, as much as there is ever a consensus in Qumran studies, would run something like this: the best archaeological evidence suggests that Qumran was a community settlement of Jews in the first century BCE and first century CE. The scrolls found in the eleven caves in the approximate vicinity of Qumran belonged to the settlement, and can be understood as a collection. However, the majority of the texts were neither composed at Qumran nor copied there, and many of them are part of the general Jewish literature of the period, rather than representative of narrow Qumran sectarian thought.[5] One group of Qumran texts affected by this reevaluation of the relationship of the texts to the site is the "Rewritten Bible" texts.

The category "Rewritten Bible" has been rather loosely defined, but the criteria for membership in this category include a close attachment, either through narrative or themes, to some book contained in the present Jewish canon of Scripture, and some type of reworking, whether through rearrangement, conflation, or supplementation, of the present canonical biblical text.[6] Thus, works such as Pseudo-Ezekiel or Pseudo-Daniel would be excluded from the category, since, although thematically related to a biblical text (Ezekiel, Daniel), they do not reuse the actual biblical text. There are three large texts from Qumran which do fit this rather loose definition: 4QReworked Pentateuch,

4   F. M. Cross, *The Ancient Library of Qumran & Modern Biblical Studies*, rev. ed., (Grand Rapids, MI: Baker Book House, 1961) p. 35 [italics mine].
5   See, e.g., J. VanderKam, *The Dead Sea Scrolls Today* (Grand Rapids, MI: Eerdmans, 1994) for a book length discussion of this general hypothesis.
6   Cf. G. Vermes, "Bible Interpretation at Qumran," in *Eretz Israel* 20 (1989) pp. 185–88.

Jubilees, and the Temple Scroll. A fourth text, the Genesis Apocryphon, also may fit this category, although, since it is in Aramaic, it is a translation as well as a rewriting.[7] In this paper I will investigate the three large texts and their relationship to one another. First, 4QReworked Pentateuch.

4QReworked Pentateuch

4QReworked Pentateuch (4QRP) appears in five manuscripts from Qumran Cave 4: 4Q158, 4Q364, 4Q365, 4Q366 and 4Q367.[8] The manuscripts preserve portions of the Torah from Genesis through Deuteronomy. As Emanuel Tov has stated in the *editio princeps,* the base text, where it can be determined for 4Q364 and probably 4Q365, was the proto-Samaritan text (that is, the recension of the Torah which is preserved, with minor ideological changes, in the Samaritan Pentateuch),[9] but 4QRP is characterized by further reworkings of the text, most notably the regrouping of passages, often, but not always, according to a common theme and by the addition of previously unknown material into the text. Two examples will suffice:

7   Other small texts may belong to this category as well, such as 4QParaphrase on Genesis and Exodus, and the pseudo-Jeremiah manuscripts.

8   J. M. Allegro, "Qumran Cave 4: I (4Q158–4Q186)" in *Discoveries in the Judaean Desert* V (Oxford: Clarendon, 1968) pp. 1–6; plate 1. E. Tov and S. White, "Reworked Pentateuch," in *Discoveries in the Judaean Desert* XIII (Oxford: Clarendon, 1994) 187–352, pls. XIII–XXXVI. M. Segal has recently argued that 4Q158 should not be classified as a manuscript of 4QRP, but as a separate composition. See his forthcoming paper, "4QReworked Pentateuch or 4QPentateuch?" in *The Dead Sea Scrolls—Fifty Years After Their Discovery*. I have not yet been able to study his argument in detail. However, the five manuscripts presently classified as 4QRP certainly represent the same type of composition/redaction.

9   E. Tov, DJD 8, pp. 192–96.

in 4Q367, frags. 2a-b, the following pericopes are grouped together: Lev 15:14–15; 19:1–4, 9–15.

> ...to the opening of the t[ent of meeting, and he will give them to the priest. (15) And the priest will make one] sin-offering and one burnt-offering, [and the priest will atone for him before the Lord for his flux. (19:1) And] the Lord [spoke] to Moses, say[ing, (2) "Speak to all the congregation of the children of Israel, and] say to them, [You will be holy, for I, the Lord you]r[God am holy.] (3) A man [will fear] his mother[and his father, and my Sabbath you will observe; I am the Lord] your[G]o[d.] (4) Do not t[urn to idols and molten gods do not make for yourselves; I am the Lord yo]ur[God.] (9) [And when you reap the harvest of your land, do not harvest com]pl[etely the border of] your field,[and do not pick the gleaning of your harvest. (10) And your vineyard do not glean, and the fallen grapes of your vineyard you must not gather] up; for the p[oor and the stranger you shall leave them; I am the Lord your God. (11) Do not steal, and do not dece]ive, and let no one l[ie to his fellow (12) or swear falsely by my name for falsehood, lest you profane]the name of your God;[I am the Lord. (13) Do not oppress your companion, and do not rob; do not keep] his wages until morni[ng. (14) Do not curse a deaf person or put a stumbling block before a blind one; you will fear] your [G]od; I[am the Lord. (15) You will not make an unjust judgment; you will not raise the face of the poor nor honor] the face of the grea[t in righteousness..."

The reason for this grouping is not immediately evident, since the passages are not thematically related (other than by being legal material), and the catchphrase "I am the Lord" appears only in the last two units. It is possible that the intervening material has been moved elsewhere in the text (Lev 18:25–29 occurs in 4Q365, frag. 22), and we are left with this rather truncated text.[10]

---

10   E. Tov and S. White, DJD 8, pp. 348–49.

An example of an addition occurs in 4Q365, frag. 23, following Lev 24:2, where at least eight additional lines of text have been inserted, which discuss festival offerings, in particular the Passover offerings and the non-biblical New Oil and Wood festivals.[11]

4.   . . . saying, when you come to the land which
5.   I am giving to you for an inheritance, and you dwell upon it securely, you will bring wood for a burnt offering and for all the wo[r]k of
6.   [the H]ouse which you will build for me in the land, to arrange it upon the altar of burnt-offering, and the calv[es
7.   ] for Passover sacrifices and for whole burnt-offerings and for thank offerings and for free-will offerings and for burnt-offerings, daily [
8.   ] and for the doors and for all the work of the House the[y] (or: he) will br[ing
9.   ] the [fe]stival (or appointed time) of fresh oil. They will bring wood two [by two
10.   ] the ones who bring on the fir[st] day, Levi [
11.   Reu]ben and Simeon and [on t]he fou[rth] day [

In neither case, nor in any of the other reworkings of the biblical text, is there any scribal indication that this is changed or new material.[12] As Michael Fishbane has noted for the phenomenon generally, in texts containing inner-biblical exegesis, there is no clear separation between lemmas and commentary.[13] In fact, for the second example given above, the terms "lemma" and "commentary" are misleading, for the additional material in frag. 23 in no way comments on the preceding "biblical" verses, but simply

---

11   E. Tov and S. White, DJD 8, pp. 290–96.
12   Of course, all five manuscripts are fragmentary, so this claim is not absolutely certain.
13   M. Fishbane, *Biblical Interpretation in Ancient Israel* (Oxford: Clarendon, 1985) p. 12.

inserts new text, presumably to give these new festivals of Oil and Wood the same force of Mosaic authority as other festivals. Therefore, it seems clear that the reader of this text was expected to view it as a text of the Pentateuch, not a "changed Pentateuch," or a "Pentateuch plus additions." In other words, if one were to place 4QReworked Pentateuch on a continuum of pentateuchal texts, the low end of the continuum would contain the shorter, unexpanded texts such as 4QDeut^g; next would be a text such as 4QExod^a; next the expanded texts in the proto-Samaritan tradition such as 4QpaleoExod^m and 4QNum^b, as well as other expanded texts not necessarily in the proto-Samaritan tradition; and then finally the most expanded text of all, 4QReworked Pentateuch.[14]

In regard to the question of whether 4QRP is sectarian, that is, peculiar to the Qumran community, the only argument in favor of this is the fact that, before its discovery in Cave 4, it was unknown in Jewish tradition. However, as is now clear, that in itself is not a sufficient argument for Qumran composition. 4QRP itself gives no internal indication of its date of composition; the earliest copy is from the first half of the second century BCE, so it must have been composed before that. Further, 4QRP shows a relationship with two texts, Jubilees and the Temple Scroll, which argue for its pre-Qumran composition. Next I shall turn to Jubilees.

Jubilees

Jubilees, which was found in fourteen or fifteen copies in five caves at Qumran,[15] is an extensive reworking of Genesis 1 – Exodus 12 that presupposes and advocates the use of the 364-day solar calendar. The author of Jubilees wished

14   For a discussion of the related question of whether or not
      the Qumran community considered 4QRP authoritative,
      see my forthcoming article "The Rewritten Bible at Qum-
      ran: A Look at Three Texts," *Israel Exploration Journal.*
15   J. VanderKam, "The Jubilees Fragments from Qumran
      Cave 4" in *The Madrid Qumran Congress: Proceedings of the*

to show that the solar calendar and the religious festivals and halakhah (and his particular interpretation of them) were not only given to Moses on Sinai, but were presupposed in the creation of the universe and carried out in the antediluvian and patriarchal history.[16] For example, in Jubilees 6, Noah is credited with being the first human to celebrate the festival of Shevuot. The author of Jubilees follows the chronological sequence of his base text, but rewrites it by adding extensive new material, such as the tales of Abraham's youth in chapter 12, and by condensing or omitting material (sometimes for ideological reasons), such as the rather shady story of Abraham passing his wife off as his sister, not once but twice (Gen 12:10–20, 20:2–7)! The author also adds supplementary or explanatory material to his biblical base text. The result is a text radically different from the Torah; it would be impossible for a reader familiar with both not to know that Jubilees was a new work. Jubilees differs in this regard from 4QRP, which a reader might accept as a text of the Torah.

There is little doubt that Jubilees was an authoritative text for the group at Qumran that preserved it. It is cited by name in the *Damascus Document* (CD) 16:3–4 and probably alluded to in CD 10:8–10. It also presents itself as an authority; the fragments from Qumran make clear that Jubilees claims to be dictated by an angel of the presence to Moses.[17] Thus, since the book both wishes to be seen as divinely inspired and is granted community acceptance as an authority, it is probable that Jubilees had authoritative

International Congress on the Dead Sea Scrolls, Madrid, 18–21 March 1991, vol. 2, J. Trebolle Barrera and L. Vegas Montaner, eds. (Leiden: Brill, 1992) p. 648.

16   For a convenient English translation of Jubilees, see O. S. Wintermute, "Jubilees" in *The Old Testament Pseudepigrapha*, vol. 2, edited by J. H. Charlesworth (New York: Doubleday, 1985) pp. 35–142.

17   J. VanderKam, "The Jubilees Fragments from Qumran Cave 4" pp. 646–47.

status at Qumran. It is generally accepted, however, that Jubilees was not composed at Qumran, since it is dated by a majority of scholars to the middle of the second century BCE, just after the Maccabaean revolt.[18] This generally accepted date may be helpful in determining 4QRP's provenance, since it is possible that in Jubilees 27 we find an allusion to 4QRP. This allusion occurs in 4Q364, frag. 3, col. 1, in the story of Jacob and Esau. 4QRP is here expanded, probably (although the text is not extant) after Gen 28:5: "And Isaac sent Jacob, and he went to Paddan Aram to Laban, the son of Bethuel the Aramean, brother of Rebekah the mother of Jacob and Esau." The expansion, for which we do not possess the beginning, concerns Rebekah's grief over the departing Jacob and Isaac's consolation of her. The text then continues with Gen 28:6.

1. him you shall see [
2. you shall see in peace [
3. your death, and to your eyes [. . . lest I be deprived of even]
4. the two of you. And [Isaac] called [to Rebecca his wife and he told]
5. her all these wor[ds
6. after Jacob her son [and she cried
7. And Esau saw that [

The expansion found here in 4QRP echoes a similar expansion in Jubilees 27, where Rebekah grieves after her departing son and Isaac consoles her. In 4Q364 the phrases in question are "him you shall see" (אותו תראה, 1.1), "you shall see in peace" (תראה בשלום, 1.2), and "after Jacob her son" (אחרי יעקוב בנה, 1.6), which recall Jub 27:14 and 17: "the spirit of Rebecca grieved after her son," and "we see him in peace" (unfortunately, these verses are not found in the Hebrew fragments of Jubilees

18   See O. S. Wintermute, "Jubilees" pp. 43–44.

found at Qumran[19]). Both texts also contain a reminiscence of Gen 27:45, "why should I be deprived of both of you in one day?" The passages in 4QRP and Jubilees are similar but not parallel. Is one alluding to or quoting the other? It seems possible, especially since this particular expansion does not occur in other reworked biblical texts (e.g. Pseudo-Philo). Further, it seems more likely that Jubilees is alluding to 4QRP than the other way around, since Jubilees is a much more systematic and elaborate reworking of the Pentateuch than 4QRP, which has here simply expanded two biblical verses. However, it is also possible that Jubilees and 4QRP are both borrowing from a common fund of tradition; a similar scene occurs in Tob 5:18–22, where Tobit and Anna are bidding farewell to Tobias. The texts would then be only indirectly related. If, however, Jubilees has used 4QRP as a source, this would indicate that 4QRP's date of composition is earlier than the mid-second century BCE date of Jubilees, and thus it cannot be a Qumran composition. The next piece of evidence in that regard comes from the Temple Scroll.

The Temple Scroll

The Temple Scroll, found in two copies from Cave 11 and two (possible) different recensions from Cave 4,[20] is a reworking of parts of the biblical text from Exodus through Deuteronomy, with a clear ideology that embraces the solar

19   J. VanderKam and J. T. Milik, "Jubilees" in DJD 13, pp. 1–186, pls. I-XII.

20   11QTemple[a]: Y. Yadin, *The Temple Scroll*, 3 vols., rev. Eng. ed. (Jerusalem: Israel Exploration Society, 1983). 11QTemple[b]: F. García Martínez, "11QTemple[b]: A Preliminary Publication," in *The Madrid Qumran Congress: Proceedings of the International Congress on the Dead Sea Scrolls, Madrid, 18–21 March 1991*, vol. 2, J. Trebolle Barrera and L. Vegas Montaner; eds. (Leiden: Brill, 1992) pp. 363–92. 4QTemple?: S. White, "4QTemple?" in DJD 13. 4Q542: E. Puech, "Fragments du plus ancien exemplaire du *Rouleau*

calendar and advocates a particular interpretation of the halakhah involving purity, festivals, and the law of the king, combined with a vision of the ideal temple. The Temple Scroll has been the subject of much controversy regarding its status and function at Qumran, illustrating my earlier point about the archaeological context of the scrolls clouding the question of their place in the literature of the Second Temple. Yigael Yadin, the editor of the Temple Scroll, stated unequivocally that "it is my considered view that the Temple scroll is undoubtedly a literary and religious product of the Dead Sea Scrolls sect."[21] Others have sharply disagreed with this assessment. Hartmut Stegemann, for example, states that "there is no specific connection whatsoever between the Qumran community and the composition of the text represented by the Temple Scroll."[22] It is certainly true that many of the ideas found in the Temple Scroll were congenial to the Qumran community, such as the solar calendar, the festivals of new wine and new oil, and the observance of strict laws of purity. However, it lacks the isolationist tone of later sectarian documents; it rather lays out a program which "includes the whole of Israel as a homogenous entity."[23] This difference makes it less likely that it was actually composed at Qumran. Further, it is certain that at least some of its sources, which include the book of Deuteronomy, were composed before the settlement at

du Temple (4Q542)" in *Legal Texts and Legal Issues: Proceedings of the Second Meeting of the International Organization for Qumran Studies, Cambridge 1995*, M. Bernstein, F. García Martínez, and J. Kampen, eds. (Leiden: Brill, 1997) pp. 19–66.

21   Y. Yadin, *The Temple Scroll: The Hidden Law of the Dead Sea Sect* (New York: Random House, 1985) p. 234.

22   H. Stegemann, "The Literary Composition of the Temple Scroll and its Status at Qumran," in *Temple Scroll Studies*, G. Brooke, ed. (Sheffield: JSOT Press, 1989) pp. 127–28.

23   G. Boccaccini, *Beyond the Essene Hypothesis* (Grand Rapids: Eerdmans, 1998) p. 103.

Qumran, although its final redaction may have taken place as late as the first century BCE.[24] Finally, it is a matter of some doubt that the Temple Scroll carried any authoritative status at Qumran (unlike Jubilees). All of these factors indicate that the Temple Scroll is a non-Qumranic composition.[25]

If the Temple Scroll is indeed a non-Qumranic composition, this is further evidence that 4QRP i. as well, since there is one indication in the Temple Scroll of dependence on or an allusion to 4QRP. This occurs in 4Q365, frag. 23, the text of which is given above, where, following Lev 24:2, the text has a long addition concerning festival offerings, including the festival of fresh oil and the wood festival, festivals also found in the Temple Scroll. In fact, as was first noted in print by Yadin, material in frag. 23 is parallel to cols. 23–24 of the Temple Scroll.[26] The decisive parallel, which points to a definite relationship, is the order of the tribes bringing the wood for the Wood Festival: Levi and Judah, Benjamin and Ephraim and Manasseh, Reuben and Simeon, Issachar and Zebulon, Gad and Asher, and Dan and Naphtali, an order which occurs only here 4QRP, in

24   See A. M. Wilson and L. Wills, "Literary Sources in the Temple Scroll," *HTR* 75 (1982) pp. 275–288; M. Hengel, J. H. Charlesworth, M. Dayagi Mendels, "The Polemical Character of 'On Kingship' in the 'Temple Scroll'. An Attempt at Dating 11QTemple," *JJS* 37 (1986) pp. 28–38; M. O. Wise, *A Critical Study of the Temple Scroll from Qumran Cave 11*, SAOC 49 (Chicago: Oriental Institute, 1990); F. García Martínez, "Sources et rédaction du Rouleau du Temple," *Henoch* 13 (1991) pp. 219–232.

25   For a discussion of the enigmatic character of the Temple Scroll, see L. Schiffman, *Reclaiming the Dead Sea Scrolls* (Philadelphia and Jerusalem: The Jewish Publication Society, 1994) pp. 257–271.

26   Y. Yadin, *The Temple Scroll*, vol. 2, rev. Eng. ed. (Jerusalem: Israel Exploration Society, 1983) p. 103.

the Temple Scroll, and nowhere else.[27] The question of concern is whether one text is citing or alluding to the other. John Strugnell, the original editor of 4QRP, suggested the possibility,[28] and Stegemann has argued outright that 4QRP is a source for the Temple Scroll.[29] Michael Wise believed that frag. 23, for which he did not have the context of 4QRP, was part of his "D Source" for the Temple Scroll.[30] Wise, in fact, argues that the additional material in frag. 23 is "deuteronomizing," an attempt to update Leviticus by the inclusion of deuteronomic language and concerns.[31] This is precisely the kind of activity we would expect in such an expanded text as 4QRP, exegesis within the text, in this case by expansion, to bring it into agreement with contemporary practice (or ideal practice), rather than overt exegesis (i.e. lemma plus commentary). Thus, it once again seems most reasonable to argue from the simpler to the more complex: The Temple Scroll, a more thorough reworking of the Torah with a clear ideological bias, has borrowed material from the expansionistic 4QRP.[32] Thus, we have two possible examples of the use of 4QRP as a source by pre-Qumranic compositions, leading to the conclusion that 4QRP was also composed prior to the settlement at Qumran.

27   For a detailed discussion of this parallel, see my article "Three Fragments from Qumran Cave 4 and their Relationship to the Temple Scroll," *JQR* 85 (1994) pp. 259–73.
28   As quoted by B. Z. Wacholder, *The Dawn of Qumran* (Cincinnati: Hebrew Union College, 1983) pp. 205–206.
29   H. Stegemann, "The Literary Composition," p. 135.
30   M. Wise, *A Critical Study* pp. 58–59.
31   M. Wise, *A Critical Study* pp. 48–50.
32   Of course, one could argue, as also in the Jubilees example, that both were drawing on a common source. That source, however, is hypothetical. See M. Wise, *A Critical Study*, chap. 2.

4QReworked Pentateuch, the Temple Scroll, and Jubilees form a constellation of texts preserved by the Qumran community. All three are closely related to the Torah, 4QRP as the product of scribal intervention for the purpose of exegesis, the Temple Scroll and Jubilees as more thorough reworkings with theological agendas. All three also present themselves as authoritative texts: 4QRP gives no indication that it is not a regular Torah text, carrying with it Mosaic authority; Jubilees claims to have been dictated to Moses by an Angel of the Presence, and the Temple Scroll presents God speaking in the first person to Moses. They bear more in common as well: 4QRP and the Temple Scroll both mention the Fresh Oil festival and the Wood festival in their legal sections, while the 364-day solar calendar advocated by Jubilees is presupposed by the Temple Scroll.[33] Finally, as stated above, it is possible that both the Temple Scroll and Jubilees draw on 4QRP as a source. As Vanderkam has stated concerning Jubilees and the Temple Scroll, "the authors of the two are drawing upon the same exegetical, cultic tradition."[34] To these two texts, I would add 4QRP. This common tradition, evidenced by three major texts found at Qumran but not composed there, is further evidence that the manuscripts from Qumran are neither eclectic, with no principal of selection, nor sectarian, reflecting the interests of an isolated, "fringe" group of Jews from the late Second Temple period, but a collection, drawn from the vast and previously unknown literature of the Second Temple period, which reflects the theological tendency of a particular group, some of whom at least resided at Qumran during the Second Temple period.[35]

33   J. VanderKam, "The Temple Scroll and the Book of Jubilees," in *Temple Scroll Studies*, G. Brooke, ed. (Sheffield: JSOT Press, 1989) p. 216.

34   J. VanderKam, "The Temple Scroll and the Book of Jubilees," p. 232.

35   See now Gabriele Boccaccini and his thesis concerning Enochic Judaism and the Essenes.

This kind of textual work demonstrates the major trend in Qumran textual studies today, a trend that goes hand-in-hand with the reevaluation of the archaeological evidence from Qumran. Together, the two disciplines of textual studies and archaeology can work to form a new synthesis in Dead Sea Scrolls studies, which will carry us forward into the twenty-first century.

Dualism at Qumran
New Perspectives

Devorah Dimant

O ne of the most striking elements in the Qumranic documents is the dualistic doctrine expounded by them. Unique in Early Judaism, this doctrine drew the attention of scholars from the earliest days of Qumran research. It was soon recognized to constitute one of the major components of the religious worldview particular to the Qumran Community, since among the Qumran documents it is recorded only in the Community's writings. The presence or absence of dualism has thus become one of the hallmarks of texts produced by the Qumran Community, as distinguished from other documents found in the library of Qumran. Although sporadic dualistic elements are to be found in other Jewish works, Qumranic as well as non-Qumranic, especially in the Aramaic apocalypses discovered at Qumran, they do not use the dualistic terminology typical of the Community's writings, such as "the Spirits of Light" and "the Spirit of Darkness." Nor do they form a comprehensive dualistic system. So the presence of such dualistic elements should be distinguished from the full-fledged sectarian dualism of the Community's writings.

The most articulate accounts of this dualistic doctrine are found in the *Rule of the Community* (1QS 3.13 through col. 4) and in the *War Rule* (1QM13.7–18). Especially detailed is the 1QS passage, labeled the *Treatise on the Two Spirits*. It offers a concise description of the created world and its operative principles, set down in abstract terms, one of the earliest examples of its kind in Jewish ancient literature. For over thirty years, this account has served as the basis for understanding and describing Qumranic dualism.[1]

During the first decades of the Qumran research, this dualistic doctrine was repeatedly discussed, often in conjunction with its assumed origins and background. Yet, the perspective of origins is different from that of content and structure. In the following discussion, these two issues will be kept apart. The problem of origins—be they Iranian,[2] or

1   See, for instance, the surveys of M. Burrows, *The Dead Sea Scrolls* (New York: Viking Press, 1955) pp. 257–58; J. M. Allegro, *The Dead Sea Scrolls* (London: Pelican, 1956) pp. 124–26, and more recently my own survey in "Qumran Sectarian Literature," *Jewish Writings of the Second Temple Period*, M. E. Stone, ed., *CRJNT* (Assen: Van Gorcum, 1984) pp. 533–4. In recent surveys, there is a tendency to play down dualism. Cf. G. Vermes, *The Dead Sea Scrolls in Perspective* (Glasgo: Collins, 1977) pp. 171–2; F. García Martínez and J. Trebolle Barera, *The People of the Dead Sea Scrolls* (Leiden: E. J. Brill, 1995) pp. 214–6; J. C. VanderKam, *The Dead Sea Scrolls Today* (Grand Rapids: Eerdmans, 1994) pp. 110–11, 182–3; L. Schiffman, *Reclaiming the Dead Sea Scrolls* (Philadelphia: Jewish Publication Society, 1996) pp. 149–50.

2   See K. G. Kuhn, "Die Sektenschrift und die iranische Religion," *ZTK* 49 (1952) pp. 296–316; A. Dupont Sommer, "Le problème des influences étrangères sur lasecte de Qumrân," *RHPR* 35 (1955) pp. 133–47; D. Winston, "The Iranian Component in the Bible, Apocrypha, and Qumran: A Review of the Evidence," *History of Religions* 5 (1966) pp. 183–216; S. Shaked, " Qumran and Iran: Further Considerations," *IOS* 2 (1972) pp. 433–46.

a result of an inner Jewish development[3]—will not be our concern here. The analysis will concentrate upon Qumranic dualism in the form known from the Qumran documents.[4]

At the early stages of the research of the Qumran documents, dualism was viewed as one, coherent system of thought. But, due to the variety of formulations found in the Community's literature, there has been a tendency to detect in the documents more than one form or pattern of dualism.[5] Some have even affirmed that the Qumranic

3   Along such lines argue, for instance, P. von der Osten-Sacken, *Gott und Belial* (Göttingen: Vandenhoeck & Ruprecht, 1969) pp. 88–169; J. Duhaime, "Le dualisme de Qumran et la littérature de sagesse vétérotestamentaire," *Église et Théologie* 19 (1988) pp. 401–22; A. Lange, *Weisheit und Prädestination* STDJ 18 (Leiden: E. J Brill, 1995); J. Frey, "Different Patterns of Dualistic Thought in the Qumran Library," *Legal Texts and Legal Issues*, M. Bernstein, F. García Martínez, and J. Kampen, eds., STDJ 23 (Leiden: Brill, 1997) pp. 274–335.

4   Of the various definitions of dualism recently proposed, I find the one advanced by Ugo Bianchi the most appropriate, especially for Qumran, since it makes the proper distinction between real dualism and mere pairs of oppositions. Bianchi rightly emphasizes that not every duality or polarity is dualistic. A pair of oppositions "is dualistic only when these oppositions are understood as principles or causes of the world and its constitutive elements." See Bianchi, "Dualism," *Encyclopedia of Religion*, vol. 4, M. Eliade, ed. (New York: Macmillan, 1987) pp. 506–12. A similar definition is offered by Z. Werblowsky, "Dualism," *EncJud*, vol. 6, p. 242.

5   Two papers which had impact in this respect are those by J. H. Charlesworth, "A Critical Comparison of the Dualism in 1QS 3:13 – 4:26 and the 'Dualism' contained in the Gospel of John," *John and Qumran*, J. H. Charlesworth, ed. (London: Geoffrey Chapman, 1971) pp. 76–106, and the more general discussion of J. G. Gammie, "Spatial and Ethical Dualism in Jewish Wisdom and Apocalyptic

texts which actually evince dualism are few and that this doctrine therefore had limited impact on the Community's worldview.[6] First of all, the claim that several dualistic patterns or stages of Qumran dualism may be discerned often rests on questionable source-criticism and dubious conclusions, a full critique of which is beyond the scope of the present paper.[7] Suffice it to say here that the variety of dualistic formulations in the Qumranic documents does not necessarily imply different patterns of dualism. The nature of these formulations suggests that they are due to different contexts and styles. As for the claim that dualism figures only in a handful of Qumran manuscripts, two observations should be made: First of all, only the sectarian manuscripts, which form a quarter of the eight hundred Qumran documents, are pertinent to dualism, since biblical and non-sectarian texts, which form the remaining share of the library, are not expected to contain dualism. In

> Literature," *JBL* 93 (1974) pp. 356–85. Subsequent discussions took up the typology used by them. Cf. e.g., H. Lichtenberger, *Studien zum Menschenbild in Texten der Qumrangemeinde* (Göttingen: Vandenhoeck & Ruprecht, 1980) pp. 190–92; Duhaime, "Le dualisme"; Frey, "Different Patterns," pp. 271, 288. Nonetheless, the multiple dualistic "patterns" claimed to be discerned are often mere oppositions rather than real dualism.

6   Frey, "Different Patterns" pp. 277–8 has recently argued that out of the eight hundred Qumranic manuscripts, only fifteen actually express dualism.

7   Lange, *Weisheit*, p. 128, and Frey, "Different Patterns," p. 296, arrive at the surprising conclusion that the *Treatise on the Two Spirits* is pre-Essene and secondary in the Community's ideology. Among others, they base this on the fact that the *Treatise on the Two Spirits* is absent from two Cave 4 copies of the *Rule of the Community* (4Q258, 4Q259). However, not only does this not necessarily lead to their conclusion, but it may be argued that as many—and some as old—Cave 4 copies of the *Rule* do include the *Treatise*.

this reduced group, dualism is present in major and important sectarian texts, and is referred to by other sectarian documents. Second, the absence of dualistic references from some of the sectarian writings does not mean that this doctrine was unknown to their authors.[8]

In light of the above considerations, it seems to me that the initial picture of Qumranic dualism still stands. Dualism will therefore be treated here as one coherent system of central importance to the Qumran Community. Furthermore, I hope to show that some facets of the Qumranic worldview usually not associated with dualism can and should be understood in a dualistic context. In fact, they acquire their full significance only within the framework of the dualistic doctrine.

Struck by the abstract tenor of 1QS 3–4, scholars have tended to understand Qumranic dualism in moralistic, abstract terms. Such interpretations view the dualistic struggle between Light and Darkness as a literary image or metaphor.[9] But, by adopting such an approach, they completely miss the concrete, material aspects of this dualism, and fail to recognize its links to other facets of the Qumran community social world and literary product. In fact, the moralistic, abstract interpretation of dualism leaves major aspects of the Qumranic life and thought, such as the religious law and calendar, outside the doctrinal framework of dualism and predestination. Thus for instance, it has never been asked whether there was any connection between the solar calendar adopted by the Qumranites and the strict dualism espoused by them. As an all-embracing principle divinely preordained, the dualistic configuration may be

8   Were we to judge by the same argument, the sectarian
     discipline, fully presented only by the *Rule of the Community*, we would have been compelled to deny sectarian
     authorship of most of the sectarian literature.
9   Cf. for instance, Duhaime, "Le dualisme," pp. 406–7;
     Frey, "Different Patterns," pp. 294, 300.

assumed to also underlie the physical cosmic order, at least in domains related to the sphere of human activity, since, according to the *Treatise on the Two Spirits* (1QS 3.18–26; cf. 4Q180 1.1–2), this sphere is the real scene of the dualistic struggle. The temporal sequence as expressed by the calendar, and by history, must therefore be subjected to this principle too, as indeed is stated by the *Rule of the Community* (1QS 3.13, 22–23; 4.15–16; 10.1–2). New texts which have recently come to light are far more articulate in this respect, and permit us to see the links between dualism, calendrical chronometry, and historical chronology.

It is now well confirmed by a number of texts that the Qumran Community adhered to a 364-day solar calendar that regulated its liturgical and cultic life.[10] The sectarian polemic against the erroneous calendar practiced by the majority of Israel (note CD 3.13–16; 6.18–19)[11] was directed against the lunar calendar enforced in the Temple of Jerusalem and adopted by most of Israel. That the problem of the calendar was of crucial importance for determining the date of the annual festivals is evident, and has long been recognized as the cause of conflicts among various groups in Israel prior to the fixation of the lunar calendar as binding.[12] However, it has never been suggested that the calendar controversy had theological implications beyond the question of fixing the dates of the cultic cycle. Such implications are clearly expressed by several new texts.

10   The following texts mention or refer to the solar calendar: 11Ps[a] 27.6–7; *Songs of the Sabbath Sacrifice* (4Q400–407, 11Q17); 11QT 21.12–28; 4Q394 (4QMMT[a]) 1–2 I-v 1–16; *4Q Calendrical Documents* A-H (4Q320–330), as well as 4Q331 and 4Q334.

11   Cf. also *Jubilees* 1:14; 6:23–38.

12   Cf. 1QpHab I, 4–8 and the classical analysis of S. Talmon, "Yom Hakippurim in the Habakkuk Scroll," *The World of Qumran from Within* (Jerusalem: Magnes, 1989) pp. 186–99. Note also 4QpHos ii 15–17 and M. J. Bernstein, "'Walking in the Festivals of the Gentiles': 4QpHosea[a] 2:15–17 and *Jubilees* 6:34–38," *JSP* 9 (1991) pp. 21–31.

Let us first consider 4Q503, published by Maurice Baillet some years ago.[13] This text records the daily evening and morning prayers to be recited by the members of the Community. Baillet recognized that the prayers conform to the solar calendar of 364 days. He also noted that the morning prayers were arranged according to the position of the sun each day, marked by the number of gates of light through which the sun enters that morning. By contrast, the evening prayers refer to a number of portions of darkness, apparently related to the lunar visibility during the monthly waning and waxing. Thus, the monthly cycle of lunar increasing and decreasing luminosity is synchronized with the annual diurnal light. In other words, the prayers correspond to the relative quantity of diurnal and nocturnal brightness. There must, then, have existed different morning and evening prayers for every single day and night in the entire annual cycle, since the relationship between diurnal and nocturnal brightness varies from one day to another.

Baillet also makes the remark that the description of the solar course as traversing heavenly gates, synchronized with the lunar monthly cycle, is similar to the lunisolar synchronism proposed by the *Astronomical Book (1 Enoch 72–76)*. The *Astronomical Book* was discovered at Qumran in four copies (4Q208–211), containing an Aramaic version more elaborate than the one preserved in the Ethiopic version of *1 Enoch*.[14]

The emphasis laid by the daily blessings of 4Q503 on the natural cycle of increasing and decreasing light, acquires its full meaning in conjunction with two other texts. The *Calendrical Document A* (4Q320),[15] and the *Calendrical*

---

13 In DJD 7, pp. 105–36. See also D. T. Olson, "Daily Prayers," in the PTSDSS Project, vol. 4A, pp. 235–85.
14 Partly published by J. T. Milik, *The Books of Enoch* (Oxford: Clarendon, 1976) pp. 273–97.
15 Partly published by J. T. Milik, "Le travail d'édition des manuscrits de Désert de Juda," VTSup 4 (1957) p. 25.

Document B (4Q321). 4Q321, published by Talmon and Knohl,[16] gives two rosters. One lists the days following the night on which the full moon begins to wane, and the days following the night of the moon's total eclipse. In other words, this list gives the monthly dates of the lowest and highest points of the lunar brightness, which correspond to the middle and the beginning of the lunar months. The other roster enumerates the first day in every solar month together with the dates of the annual festivals, and specifies the term of the priestly course in which each festival falls. The manner in which the *Calendrical Document B* links the festivals to longer days and bright nights indicates that such days and nights were seen as auspicious, whereas dark nights were considered evil. In the words of the editors of this text, "The moon is portrayed as a source of the dark days of evil. In contrast, the sun is seen as the fountainhead of holy and blessed days, the first days of the months and all the festival, as determined by the solar calendar."[17] Here, an explicit link is established between the light and the propitious, holy festivals. Such a link is meaningful only if the light is perceived as the material emanation of the good.

Light is viewed as beneficial also by the Hebrew cryptic text of 4Q186.[18] Named by its first editor "a horoscope," it

16   S. Talmon and I. Knohl, "A Calendrical Scroll from a Qumran Cave: *Mišmarot* Bª, 4Q321," *Pomegranates Golden Bells: Studies in Biblical, Jewish and Near Eastern Ritual, Law, and Literature in Honor of Jacob Milgrom*, D. P. Wright, D. N. Freedman, and A. Hurvitz, eds. (Winona Lake: Eisenbrauns, 1995) pp. 276–302. In an earlier, preliminary version, it was published by B.-Z. Wacholder and M. G. Abegg, *A Preliminary Edition of the Unpublished Dead Sea Scrolls*, vol. 1 (Washington: Biblical Archaeology Society, 1991) 1:60–75.

17   Talmon and Knohl, "A Calendrical Scroll," (n. 16) p. 299.

18   Published by J. M. Allegro, *Qumran Cave 4.I*, DJD 5, pp. 88–91. See the corrections by J. Strugnell, "Notes en marge du Volume V des 'Discoveries in the Judaean Desert of Jordan,'" *RQ* 7 (1970) pp. 274–6.

is, however, an astrological physiognomy[19] that describes
the physical qualities of persons born under particular
zodiacal signs. In order to decide the nature of the person's
"spirit" (ruaḥ), namely his or her nature in terms of light
and darkness, this text calculates on a nine-parts scale the
number of parts "in the house of light" and the number of
parts "in the pit of darkness" allotted to persons born
under various zodiacal signs, and their respective physical
properties.[20] Such a ratio of light and darkness seems to be
apportioned to every person, a ratio which decides his or
her place in the communal hierarchy, as is indicated by the
Damascus Document (CD 13.3). Perhaps a text such as
4Q186 served as a physiognomical guide in examining the
character of new candidates to the community.[21] Be the
case as it may, 4Q186 clearly espouses the view that the portions of physical light and darkness were endowed with
ethical-metaphysical dimensions.

The terminology of "light" and "darkness" assigns
4Q186 to the Community's literature. However, physiognomy and astrology are not specific to Qumran, but were

19   See H. S. Alexander, "Physiognomy, Initiation, and Rank
     in the Qumran Community," *Geschichte-Tradition-Reflexion:
     Festschrift für Martin Hengel zum 70. Geburtstag, I-Judentum,*
     ed. P. Schäfer (Tübingen: Mohr-Siebeck, 1996) p. 385.
20   See the discussion of Lichtenberger, *Studien zum Menchen-
     bild,* pp. 142–8; F. Schmidt has recently interpreted 4Q186
     as using a system calculating the horoscope from the
     moment of conception rather than the time of birth. Cf.
     his discussion in "Astrologie juive ancienne: Essai d'inter-
     prétation de 4Qcryptique (4Q186)," *RQ* 18 (1997) pp.
     125–41. However, according to his interpretation, persons
     with more parts of light (cf. 4Q186 1 ii 7–9) are born in
     the winter, when the days are the shortest. This does not
     seem to fit with the overall Qumranic concept. It is there-
     fore preferable to see the date appearing in 4Q186 as
     referring to the actual birth.
21   As suggested by Alexander, "Physiognomy, Initiation and
     Rank," pp. 390–1.

widely practiced in antiquity.[22] Indeed, 4Q186 appears to have drawn upon Babylonian traditions, since it seems to begin the zodiac with the sign of Taurus rather than with the conventional sign of Aries. In fact, this is a particularity of certain Babylonian astrological systems.[23] In this, 4Q186 offers an interesting example of reworking older, non-Jewish traditions into the specific ideology of the Qumran Community.

The importance of physiognomy for the Community, as well as its non-Qumranic origin, are also suggested by the presence at Qumran of other physiognomic texts, all in Aramaic.[24] In fact, the use of Aramaic is one of the indications of the non-Qumranic origin, for all the explicitly sectarian works are written in Hebrew.[25]

22 Cf. H. S. Alexander, "Physiognomy, Initiation and Rank," pp. 385–94.
23 Also a selenodromion found in 4Q318 (cf. below) follows this order, which is found in the astronomical Babylonian MUL.APIN texts. Cf. M. Albani, "Der Zodiakos in 4Q318 und die Henoch-Astronomie," *Forschungsstelle Judentum, Mittelunge und Beiträge* 7 (1993) pp. 27–32; J. C. Greenfield and M. Sokoloff, "An Astrological Text from Qumran (4Q318) and Reflections of Some Zodiacal Names," *RQ* 16 (1995) pp. 507–25, esp. p. 516. In the light of these Babylonian parallels, Wise's skepticism regarding a possible connection between 4Q186 and 4Q318 is unwarranted. Cf. M. Wise, "Thunder in Gemini: An Aramaic Brontologion (4Q318) from Qumran," in *Thunder in Gemini* JSPSup 15 (Sheffield: Sheffield Academic, 1994) p. 39 n. 85.
24 4Q561 is a physiognomical text, but it does not appear to be an Aramaic copy of 4Q186, as claimed by some, for it lacks the astrological part. For edition, cf. K. Beyer, *Die aramäschen Texte vom Toten Meer—Ergänzungsband* (Göttingen: Vandenhoeck & Ruprecht, 1994) pp. 125–6. 4Q534 known as the 'Elect of God', also contains physiognomic sections. For the edition cf. Beyer, *ibid* pp. 125–6. Cf. Alexander, "Physiognomy, Initiation and Rank," pp. 393–4.
25 See my comments to the list of the Qumran manuscripts in "The Qumran Manuscripts: Contents and Significance," in

A Babylonian background is now suggested even for the Qumranic 364-day calendar. There is now evidence that, during the seventh century BCE, an ideal stellar year of 360 days was practiced, and also a mean lunar year of 364.[26] It seems that this ideal stellar 360-day year underlies the *Astronomic Book* (*1 Enoch* 72–76) and another Qumranic text, an Aramaic selenodromion (4Q318), namely, a record of the lunar monthly movement through the signs of the zodiac to help in determining fortuitous days.[27] Both works synchronize the solar course with the lunar monthly positions. Apparently, this synchronism is taken up by the prayers of 4Q503 and by the *Calendrical Document B*, and is thus adapted into the dualistic framework specific to the Community.[28]

The importance of periods of light and obscurity during daily and yearly cycles, as expressed in the above texts, throws an interesting light on Josephus's statement that the Essenes used to recite certain morning prayers facing the

Time to Prepare the Way in the Wilderness, D. Dimant and L. H. Schiffman, eds., STDJ 16 (Leiden: Brill, 1995) pp. 34–35.

26 See W. Horowitz, "The 360 and 364 Day Year in Ancient Mesopotamia," *JANES* 24 (1997) pp. 35–44.

27 For the *Astronomical Book*, see Albani, "Der Zodiakos." For 4Q318, see J. C. Greenfield and M. Sokoloff, "An Astrological Text." For late Greek parallels, cf. M. Wise, "Thunder in Gemini: An Aramaic Brontologion." 4Q318 contains also a brontologion, namely, a record of meteorological phenomena through the zodiacal signs for the purpose of prognostication, a well-known genre in antiquity. Cf. J. C. Greenfield and M. Sokoloff, "Astrological and Related Omen Texts in Jewish Palestine Aramaic," *JNES* 48 (1989) pp. 201–14; Wise, *ibid*.

28 How did these sectarian texts resolve the problem of the gap between the 360-day stellar year and the Qumranic 364-day solar year? In view of this gap, some scholars concluded that 4Q318 adopted a calendar different from the Qumranic one. Cf. e.g., J. C. Greenfield and M. Sokoloff, "An Astrological Text," pp. 511–12. However, the author of the *Astronomical Book* was perfectly aware of the

sun rising upon the horizon (*War*, ii, 128). Such a practice becomes meaningful if we assume that the Essenes recognized in the physical light a manifestation of the divine goodness and presence.

That the sequence of good and evil periods was not restricted to the annual cycle, but extended over a six-year cycle, is attested by the same *Calendrical Document*, 4Q321. Although the six-year cycle in this document is connected only with the terms of Temple service allotted to the twenty-four priestly courses, it has far-reaching implications; for the six-year cycle is an artificial scale of time, connected to a jubilees chronology and not to the natural cycle of seasons. 4Q321 thus links calendrical chronometry to chronological history.

A register of historical events according to a jubilees chronology is indeed contained in another calendrical text, the *Calendrical Document C^b* (4Q322).[29] This text calculates the terms of priestly courses in a sequence of weeks of years and jubilees. In addition it notes various events. In one fragment, Queen Shelomzion and King Hyrcanus II are mentioned (4Q322 4 4,6).[30] In another copy of the same

      problem, since he offers a way to reconcile the two computations. In his system, he does not count four days: the two soltices and the two equinoxes. See *1 Enoch* 75:1 and the notes of O. Neugebauer, "Appendix A," in M. Black, *The Book of Enoch or 1 Enoch*, SVTP 7 (Leiden: Brill, 1985) p. 394. This may well have been the solution adopted by the Qumranites. This solution would have permitted the use at Qumran of all the zodiacal calculations which were based on a 360-day year, including 4Q186. On the 364-day year as connected to intercalation of the lunar years, see Horowitz, "The 360 and 364 Day Year."

29   Cf. B.-Z. Wacholder and M. Abegg, *A Preliminary Edition*, vol. 1, pp. 77–85.

30   Alexandra Shelomzion reigned from 76 to 67 BCE, and her son Hyrcanus II reigned from 67 to 63 BCE.

work, the Roman governor Aemilius Scaurus is mentioned (4Q324ᵃ 2).[31]

The dating of historical events according to a jubilees chronology was widely used during Second Temple times. Best known among the non-Qumranic examples are the biblical Daniel 9, the biblical history as told by the *Book of Jubilees*, the *Apocalypse of Weeks* (*1 Enoch* 93, 91), the *Animal Apocalypse* (*1 Enoch* 84–90), and the *Testament of Levi* 16. All these texts were also known at Qumran. Indeed, the jubilees chronology is also used by texts known only from Qumran, such as *Pseudo-Moses* (4Q390 1),[32] as, in fact, is the basic idea of history as a sequence of definite periods (1QS 3.15; 4.13; 1QH 1.24; 1QpHab 7.13; CD 2.9–10).

Since both the 364-day calendar and the jubilees chronology appear in non-sectarian texts, they must have also been practiced by circles outside the Qumran Community. In regards to the calendar, this possibility has been recognized long ago.[33] But it seems to be the case also for the

31 Aemilius Scaurus was the Roman governor of Syria between 65–62 BCE. He was appointed by Pompey after the conquest of Jerusalem in 63 BCE.

32 See also 4Q247. For 4Q390, cf. my publication "New Light from Qumran on the Jewish Pseudepigrapha: 4Q390," in *The Madrid Qumran Congress*, vol 2, J. Trebolle Barrera and I. Vegas Montaner, eds. (Leiden: Brill, 1992) pp. 405–8. For 4Q274, see the edition of J. T. Milik, *The Books of Enoch* (Oxford: Clarendon, 1976) p. 256. On the jubilees chronology, see my discussion in "The Seventy Weeks Chronology (Dan 9:24–27) in the Light of New Qumranic Texts," in *The Book of Daniel in the Light of New Findings*, ed. A. S. Van der Woude (Leuven: University Press, 1993) pp. 37–76.

33 It has been recently suggested that 11QPsᵃ is a liturgical collection of Davidic psalms arranged according to the solar calendar and that this collection originated in non-Qumranic circles practicing that calendar. Cf. P. W. Flint, *The Dead Sea Psalms Scrolls and the Book of Psalms*, STDJ 17 (Leiden: Brill, 1997) pp. 172–201.

historical lists devised on the basis of the jubilees chronology.[34] However, the Qumranites seemed to have adopted
the jubilees chronology for their own needs and apparently
devised their own lists. Such lists served three purposes:
cultic functions, historical dating, and the practice of laws
pertaining to the sabbaths of years (*shemṭot*).[35]

The Qumranic lists are also distinctive in that they link
the jubilees chronology with the annual calendrical cycle of
light and darkness, and thus incorporated it into their
dualistic framework. They seem to have calculated periods
of "light" and "darkness," namely, good and evil, for history itself, in a manner similar to that of non-Qumranic
Jewish apocalypses.[36] This is indicated by the *Pesher on the
Periods* (4Q180), which records alternating good and evil
historical periods.[37] Such historical lists may have been

34   The presence at Qumran of calendrical records in accor-
     dance with the jubilees chronology discards the established
     view that the *Damascus Document* cites *Jubilees* (in 16.3–4:
     ". . . the Book of the Divisions of the Times in their Jubi-
     lees and in their Weeks"). This opinion was formed before
     the existence of the calendrical documents was known. In
     fact, some of the calendrical lists from Qumran, or similar
     ones which probably existed at the time, fit as well with the
     citation. Consequently, attempts at dating the *Damascus
     Document* or *Jubilees* on basis of this supposed citation
     should also be discarded.

35   That the Qumranites practiced these laws is indicated by
     4Q513 frg. 18, line 3. See also 1QM 2.6,8; 4Q496 (4QM^f)
     frg. 7, line 3.

36   Compare the *Apocalypse of Weeks* (*1 Enoch* 93:1–10;
     91:10–17); the *Animal Apocalypse* (*1 Enoch* 89:54–90); the
     Testament of Levi 16. Note *Syriac Baruch* 53, where Baruch
     sees a vision about the future which portrays good and evil
     periods as dark and bright waters.

37   Cf. my edition of 4Q180 and commentary in "The 'Pesher
     on the Periods' (4Q180) and 4Q181," *IOS* 9 (1979) pp.
     77–102. An edition and translation of 4Q180 and 4Q181
     have been recently published by J. J. M. Roberts in *The
     Dead Sea Scrolls*, vol. 2, J. H. Charlesworth, ed. (Tübingen:

used at Qumran for studying the past and foretelling the future. This would fit well with Josephus's statement that the Essenes could foretell the future (*War.* ii, 159; *Ant.* xiii, 311).

The concrete nature of the evil presence in the world is conveyed by two other Qumranic interconnected beliefs concerning sickness and demons. The notion that sickness is caused by particular demons was widespread in antiquity, but the biblical reticence to speak about this subject is well-known. Only a few obscure allusions can be detected in the biblical literature.[38] By contrast, the idea that sickness is inflicted by God or his agents as punishment of sin is a basic tenet of the biblical worldview and is repeatedly expressed.[39] The scrolls inherited the biblical notion of sickness as punishment,[40] but develop it further in several ways.

In a passage from the *Damascus Document,* preserved only in Cave 4 copies, a scale disease is attributed to a harmful spirit (4Q266 6 i 6), while the healing of the same disease is attributed to a salutary "spirit of life" (4Q266 6 i 12).[41] The term "spirit" is notoriously polyvalent in the

Mohr-Siebeck, 1995) pp. 204–13. Roberts does not seem to know my publication, for he has not taken into account my edition or my critique of J. T. Milik's thesis that 4Q180 and 4Q181 are copies of the same work. Roberts publishes the combined text as proposed by Milik, disregarding other criticism on this thesis as well (e.g., R. V. Huggins "A Canonical 'Book of Periods' at Qumran?" *RQ* 15 (1991) pp. 421–36. The original presentation of Milik's thesis was published in "Milkî-sedeq et Milkî-reša' dans les anciens écrits juifs et chrétiens," *JJS* 23 (1972) pp. 95–144: idem, *The Books of Enoch*, pp. 248–53.

38   Cf. the reference to, *deber,* "pestilence" (Hab 3:5), and Lilith (Isa 34:14), associated in the ancient Near East with child sickness. Cf. A. Caquot, "Sur quelques démons de l'A.T. (Reshep, Qeteb, deber)," *Sem* 6 (1956) pp. 53–68.
39   See, for instance, Exod 4:11; Deut 32:39; 1 Sam 5:6.
40   See 1QpHab 9.1–2; 10–12; 1QS 4.12; *Genesis Apocryphon* 20.16, 28–29.
41   4Q266 6 i; 4Q269 7; 4Q272 1 i; 4Q273 4 ii. See the edition of J. M. Baumgarten and J. T. Milik, DJD 18, p. 52,

writings of the Community, and one is inclined to connect it with the evil spirits mentioned elsewhere in the scrolls.[42] However, the passage does not lend itself to such interpretation. It does not mention demons and the phraseology of the description suggests rather the corporal nature of the "spirits," and thus indicates that they are real substances which affect the bodily condition. Indeed, the duality of spirits bringing health or causing sickness reflects the dualistic structure of the physical world. The *Damascus Document* seems to connect the notion of corporeality of the dual spirits with the idea that sickness is a punishment for sin. For the CD includes persons with leprosy in a list of transgressors.[43] Underlying is the idea that sin causes God to remove his protection from the sinner, who is thus rendered vulnerable and prone to sickness. Interestingly, the concrete nature of a maleficent demonic influence which causes sickness is asserted by another Aramaic text from Qumran, specifically 4Q560, which is probably an incantation against demons.[44] Although this text is probably not sectarian, its presence in the library shows the interest, and perhaps the use made of such incantations at Qumran.

The link between demons, sickness, and sin is given a graphic expression by the book of *Jubilees*, a work known at Qumran in no less than fifteen copies.[45] *Jubilees* accepts the

and J. M. Baumgarten, "The 4QZadokite Fragments on Skin Disease," *JJS* 41 (1990) 153–65.

42 Suggested by A. Lange, "The Essene Position on Magic and Divination," in *Legal Texts and Legal Issues*, M. Bernstein, F. García Martínez, and J. Kampen, eds., STDJ 23 (Leiden: Brill, 1997) p. 412. In similar vein is also the comment of Baumgarten, "4QZadokite Fragments," p. 162.

43 In 4Q270 2 ii 12. Cf. Baumgarten, *The Damascus Document* (n. 41) p. 144; *idem*, "The 4QZadokite Fragments," p. 162.

44 For edition, see Beyer, *Die aramaischen Texte*, pp. 129–30. See the comments of Lange, "The Essene Position," pp. 385–6.

45 A survey of the manuscripts of *Jubilees* found at Qumran are given by J. VanderKam, The *Book of Jubilees—Translation*

view expressed in *1 Enoch* 15:8–12 that the demons are the impure and malevolent spirits, issued of the dead antediluvian giants, the offspring of the unlawful union between the angels and the women. *Jubilees* 10 develops this story and links demonic activity and human sickness in a new way. It limits the demonic power in two ways. Placed under the authority of their leader Mastema, the number of active demons permitted to remain upon earth is reduced to a tenth of the original number. Moreover, the demons role in leading humanity astray is given because "great is the wickedness of men" (*Jub* 10:9). Thus, the demonic power is restricted inasmuch as demons are permitted to inflict sickness and other evils only on sinners. Finally, Noah receives from the angels antidotes for the diseases, a book of remedies. Thus, *Jubilees* places the demonic activity within the limits set by divine will, and under divine authority. Such a picture of demonic activity offers an explanation of the fear of impurity and sin, which permeates all the sectarian writings.[46] To take this worldview one step further, if the Qumranites combated sin so as to avoid demonic powers, they may have been engaged in medicine to counteract such powers once people came under their influence. In fact, Josephus attributed to the Essenes precisely this preoccupation with medicines (*War*, ii, 136).

Another means of protection against demonic powers practiced at Qumran was to recite magical songs in order to ward off the demons. Such songs are assembled in the collections of 11QPs[a] (11Q11) and the *Songs of the Maskil* (4Q510–511).[47]

CSCO 511 (Louvain: Peeters, 1989) p. vii. For Cave 4 copies, see the edition of J. T. Milik and J. VanderKam in DJD 13, pp. 1–94.

46   Phrased as a general principle in 1QS 3.22–24; 4.12–14.

47   For 11QPsAp[a] (11Q11) see E. Puech, "11QPsAp[a]: Un rituel d'exorcismes. Essai de reconstruction," *RQ* 14 (1989) 377–408; *idem*, "Les deux derniers Psaumes davidiques du rituel d'exorcisme, 11QPsAp[a] IV 4-VI 14," *The Dead Sea*

Significantly, several Qumranic documents, sectarian and non-sectarian, associate demons with darkness, and relegate them to a dark abode in the nether regions of the earth.[48] Although such association is common in antiquity, and the Qumranites drew upon older traditions, they nevertheless incorporated such demonology into their own dualistic framework,[49] in which darkness was seen as the material manifestation of the demonic, whereas light was a reflection of the divine. Consequently, when the Community took up the traditional associations of demons with the netherworld, and the angels with the heavenly abode, these two cosmic domains acquired a dualistic mien. They form

Scrolls: Forty Years of Research, D. Dimant and U. Rappaport, eds. (Leiden: Brill, 1992) pp. 64–89. For 4Q510–511, see the edition of M. Baillet, DJD 7, pp. 215–62. For discussion, see B. Nitzan, *Prayer and Religious Poetry*, STDJ 12 (Leiden: Brill, 1994) pp. 227–72.

48   In the sectarian exorcist text of 11QPs[a] (11Q11) iv 7–9, the demon described "darkness and not light" and is expected to be imprisoned in the lowest earth. Cf. Puech, "rituel d'exorcism." On underworld non-sectarian Aramaic documents, see *1 Enoch* 10:5–6 (Asael is imprisoned in the depth of earth covered with darkness); the demon Milkî-reša' is ruler of darkness whose abode is in darkness in the one section of the Aramaic *Visions of Amram* (4QvisAmr[b] [4Q544] ii 1–6; iii 1–2). For edition, see K. Beyer, *Die aramäischen Texte vom Toten Meer* (Göttingen: Vandenhoeck & Ruprecht, 1984) p. 210–14, and the remarks and translation of É. Puech, *La Croyance des Esséniens en la vie future*, vol. 2 (Paris: Gabalda, 1993) pp. 535–6.

49   As also observed by P. S. Alexander, "'Wrestling against Wickedness in High Places': Magic in the Worldview of the Qumran Community," in *The Scrolls and the Scriptures*, S. E. Porter and C. A. Evans, eds., JSPSup 26 (Sheffield: Sheffield Academic, 1997) pp. 336–8.

another pair of oppositions reflecting the fundamental dualistic structure of creation.

I hope that I have presented sufficient data to show that Qumranic dualism is the basic structural principle, not only of the angelic and human spheres, but also of the material and corporal aspects of the universe. Manifested in physical light and darkness, duality is also the principle which governs the course of calendrical and historical times. Assessing the full dimensions of Qumranic dualism will permit us to perceive new connections with Jewish apocalypticism on the one hand, and with Iranian dualism on the other hand.

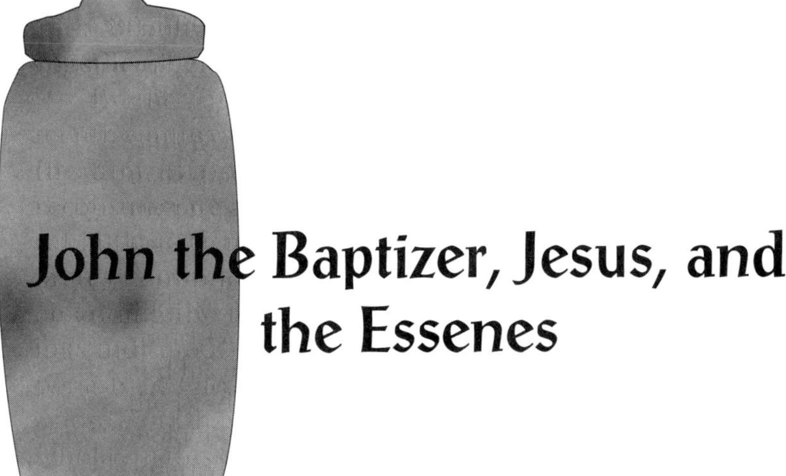

John the Baptizer, Jesus, and the Essenes

James H. Charlesworth

Introduction

Fifty years ago, Ta'âmireh Bedouin found a cave to the west of the north end of the Dead Sea. In it were the remains of a Jewish library from the time of the Second Temple. The Bedouin were disappointed at their discovery. Gold had been expected. Only smelly leather rolls were recovered.

For a long period, the value of the Dead Sea Scrolls was not seen. In the late forties, for example, they were on display in the chapel of Duke University. No one person, group, or university in the USA wanted to purchase them. As is well known, they were advertised in the *Wall Street Journal* and eventually purchased by Yigael Yadin for Israel.

The American Schools of Oriental Research played a major role in helping to discern and stress the invaluable nature of these ancient Jewish documents. They passed through numerous middlemen. From the Bedouin to Kando, to Archbishop Samuel, and finally to the building on Saladin Street then called the American School of Oriental Research. There, John C. Trever and William H. Brownlee began to discern their value. It was Professor William F. Albright who should have settled their value when he claimed that they were ancient—that is, they antedate the destruction of Jerusalem in 70 CE—and that one of the greatest of manuscript discoveries had been made. The first publications of the scrolls were in *Biblical Archaeologist*. The first fascicles of text and transcriptions of the Dead Sea Scrolls were published by the ASOR. Working efficiently behind the scene was the ASOR Ancient Manuscript Committee which formerly consisted of Cross, Freedman, Sanders, Strugnell, and myself as well as philanthropists. The committee helped guide the study and preservation of the scrolls and the attempt to acquire for scholarship additional ancient texts.

Ever since Albright's wise evaluation of the Dead Sea Scrolls, scholars have demonstrated how invaluable these scrolls are for understanding and reconstructing the world of Palestinian Judaism before 70 CE. The present review will clarify how essential they are for understanding John the Baptizer and Jesus of Nazareth.

At the outset, it is imperative for me to suggest why archaeology is now essential for New Testament research. We have come a long way since 1968 and 1969 when I was Thayer Fellow of the ASOR. I was asked why I was interested in archaeology, which really at that time was the domain of the Old Testament (Hebrew Bible) expert. These specialists rightly pointed out that their texts referred to cities, armies, international affairs, and major events that left realia and artifacts. Moreover, they correctly asserted that they worked with over a millennium of sources and archaeological evidence. The documents in the New Testament cover merely one century, at the most, and the events recorded in it were by no means seen as internationally important to their contemporaries. That is to say, the conquest of Jerusalem by the army of Nebuchadrezzar in 597 and 587 BCE would have been reported on something like

CNN, but the burning of Qumran would have scarcely made the local news.

Since the 1960s, it has become axiomatic that archaeology is important, indeed essential, for New Testament research. Let me briefly illustrate that point. Bethsaida was named Julia in 30 CE, but while Josephus knows that fact and often refers to the site by both names, the New Testament Gospels refer to it only as Bethsaida. I see that minor point as an indication of the antiquity of many traditions in the Gospels that describe events that antedate 30 CE. James and John (the sons of Zebedee) and Peter all come from Bethsaida, and Jesus refers to this city as Bethsaida, but all these events occur prior to 30. It is also conceivable that the large and wealthy fisherman's house on the main public courtyard may well have belonged to Zebedee, the father of James and John.[1]

Stone vessels are clearly demanded for the Jewish rites of purification according to the *Temple Scroll*, the longest of all the Dead Sea Scrolls. Stone vessels are now found in the palatial houses in Upper Jerusalem, at Qumran, and elsewhere. All seem to date from the time from when Herod the Great began to rebuild the Temple in 20 BCE to its burning under Titus in September 70 CE. It is wise to remember that, according to the Gospel of John, Jesus attended a wedding at Cana in which there were six jars set aside for the Jewish rites of purification. They were said to be made of stone. The event would have antedated 30 CE.

In Jerusalem, archaeological research proves that Golgotha was outside the western wall of the city in 30 or 33 and that the present western wall has a foundation constructed sometime after 40 CE. That one discovery undermines the claim that the site of the large stone in the

---

1   For a good summary of archaeological research in Bethsaida, see R. Arav and R. A. Freund, eds., *Bethsaida: A City by the North Shore of the Sea of Galilee*, Bethsaida Excavations Project 1(Kirksville, MO: Thomas Jefferson University Press, 1995).

Church of the Holy Sepulcher cannot be the stone on which Jesus was crucified because it is within the Old City. The issue concerns the location of Golgotha in relation to the western wall of Jerusalem in 30 and 33 and not today or even in 44.[2]

In Capernaum, Peter's home may well have been discovered. Looking down into the ruins, we can imagine thin walls which would be roofed with thatch so that one could dig down through them to a speaker seated below in order to let down a paralytic for healing. The small circular enclosure helps us understand that ancient social world. We are stimulated to think about a Jew who gathered around him not thousands, but only about twenty interested persons (even if others are reported to be pressing for admission from outside [see Mark 2:1–12]).

The Herodian structures at Masada, Sebaste, Caesarea Maritima, Jericho, Dan, and especially Jerusalem remind us that first-century Judaism was not cut off from the world; it was one of the majestic and advanced civilizations of Hellenistic culture. Some of the greatest engineers in the world came to the land of Herod the Great to build cities and unbelievably massive structures. They were followed by athletes, artisans, scholars, and businessmen all eager to perform and become wealthy.

These brief reminders are partial answers to those interlocutors who in the late 1960s felt that I was wasting my time being interested in archaeology. But, the greatest archaeological discovery was not even itemized in the preceding impressive list. I refer, of course, to the Dead Sea Scrolls. No library has yet been found from biblical times that can as yet rival the Dead Sea Scrolls in importance, even though many of us have heard about the possibility of

2   For fuller discussions on these points and illustrations see Charlesworth, "The Jesus of History and the Archaeology of Palestine," in *Jesus Within Judaism: New Light from Exciting Archaeological Discoveries*, Anchor Bible Reference Library 1 (New York, London: Doubleday, 1988) pp. 103–30.

a library almost unearthed at Hazor. Having made these comments, I wish to emphasize that the Dead Sea Scrolls are a treasure trove for Old Testament as well as New Testament scholars. But, it is to the period immediately antedating the New Testament documents that I shall confine my present focused reflections.

Obviously, it is not possible today, two thousand years after the events, to write a biography of John the Baptizer or of Jesus. Our sources, the New Testament documents and Josephus's works, show no interest in biographical analysis. Furthermore, they are far removed from the events they describe. The New Testament authors are more concerned in proclaiming faith in Jesus; and Josephus is primarily interested in selling the attractiveness of Judaism to Romans and Greeks and especially his benefactors, the Roman emperors, Vespasian, Titus, and Domitian.

The Essenes

There are two roads to take in assessing the importance of the Dead Sea Scrolls for a better understanding of John the Baptizer and Jesus of Nazareth. If one were to head south from Tiberias today, one would see a desert land with barbed wire fences and a little river called the Jordan becoming even less impressive. If one headed north of Tiberias one would see a sea glistening in the sun, miles of vineyards, fertile plains, and verdant fields. It does matter which road to take.

To take the road which indicates that the Qumran scrolls are not Essene leaves us with some bewilderment. How could such a significant writing group living in a symbolic area of Judea and descending from Aaron and Zadok be omitted by Josephus when he describes the groups or sects within Judaism? How could the Qumranites not be Essenes when Pliny the Elder, who died in the volcanic destruction of Pompeii in 79 CE, describes Essenes living precisely where Qumran is located?[3] How could Qumran not be Essene when almost everything we know about the Qumranites aligns impressively with what we know from Philo, Josephus, Pliny the Elder, and many others about the Essenes? To take a road that calls for caution in making such an obvious equation is laudable perhaps, but it will not take us anywhere but into the wilderness and the desert.

To follow the road that sees a relationship between the Essenes and the Qumranites opens up a veritable world for reflection. We can understand why there seems to be an Essene gate in the southwest section of first-century Jerusalem (as we know from Josephus, the *Temple Scroll*, and archaeological research). The relationship helps us comprehend Josephus's comment that there were two types of Essenes: those who were celibate and those who married. This same phenomenon seems to be represented by two of the major "sectarian" scrolls: that is, the *Rule of the Community* represents the more conservative, probably celibate, group of Essenes who lived sequestered in the wilderness preparing the Way of Yahweh while following their understanding of Isa 40:3. The *Damascus Document* then seems to represent the other group of Essenes who did marry and had more normal relations with other Jews. Likewise, we come much closer to understanding Philo's Therapeutae, who may well be related to the Essenes—that is, a form of Essenism in Alexandria. The conclusion that the Qumranites most likely represent only a branch of Essenism helps us also understand why only about 150 people, probably all men, lived at Qumran, while the report in Philo and Josephus states that four thousand Essenes lived in ancient Palestine and on the outskirts of cities or villages. Hence, most of the Essenes were not at Qumran; they were living in Jerusalem, but as far away from the Temple cult as possible and on the fringes of most cities or villages in the Holy Land.

3   Pliny the Elder, *Nat. Hist.* 5.17.4 section 73.

This, in my opinion, is the proper road to take, and virtually all specialists in Qumran research have taken it. It frees us from such errors as those committed in the past. For example, some scholars announced that Jesus could not have known and therefore was not influenced in any way by the Essenes because he never visited Qumran. Philo and Josephus place most of the Essenes in precisely the same arena in which Jesus is reported to have delivered his major parables and speeches. He usually taught on the outskirts of cities or villages. Thus, Jesus probably knew and was influenced by Essenes, even if he never visited Qumran. This is the road which will supply us with food for thought.

John the Baptizer

Since the early fifties scholars, journalists, and novelists have claimed that John the Baptizer was an Essene. They saw similarities and announced equations. They noticed parallels and declared identities. As is usually the case, the response was equally excessive. Some scholars with amazing confidence reacted and claimed that John the Baptizer was not in any way influenced by or related to the Essenes.

Scholarship should not begin nor become blinded by what is found in secondary and tertiary literature. Our research must begin and end with a struggle to understand our primary sources. Hence, I shall begin by assessing in order of importance the similarities and dissimilarities between what our sources say about John the Baptizer and about the Essenes; then I will attempt to explain these similarities and dissimilarities.

Josephus's report concerning John the Baptizer is crucial. John, according to Josephus, our historian of Early Judaism, "was a good man (ἀγαθὸν ἄνδρα) and had exhorted the Jews to lead righteous lives, to practice justice towards their fellows and piety towards God, and so doing join in baptism" (*Ant* 18.116–19).[4] It helps us see the biased presentation of him in the Gospels as merely the precursor of Jesus. John deserves to be seen as a significant figure within Second Temple Judaism.[5] It also seems likely, in light of what we read in the Fourth Gospel, that rather than merely being the forerunner of Jesus, John may well have been Jesus' teacher at the very beginning of his ministry (John 1:29–42; 3:22–24; 4:1 [4:2 is clearly redactional and later]).[6]

Similarities

A most important link between John the Baptizer and the Qumran Essenes is their preference for prophecy, especially the traditions associated with Isaiah. They often focused on Isaiah 40 and found their *raison d'être* in this chapter. According to 1QS 8.13–14, the Qumranites have separated themselves from the men of deceit "in order to depart into the wilderness (למדבר)." They will "prepare there the Way of the Lord; as it is written: 'In the wilderness (במדבר) prepare the way of the Lord, make level in the desert a highway for our God.'"[7] According to Mark, Isa 40:3 is associated with John the Baptizer who has appeared

4   For the Greek and English, see L. H. Feldman, *Josephus*, LCL 433 (Cambridge, MA: Harvard University Press, 1965) pp. 80–83.

5   This position is the strong point in J. E. Taylor's *The Immerser: John the Baptist Within Second Temple Judaism* (Grand Rapids, 1997).

6   See esp. J. P. Meier, "Jesus a Disciple of John?" in *A Marginal Jew* (New York, London: Doubleday, 1994) vol. 2, pp. 116–30. I fully agree with Meier when he states, ". . . by submitting to his message and baptism, Jesus became the disciple, the pupil, the student of the rabbi called John" (vol. 2, p. 116).

7   All translations are my own, unless otherwise noted. For a discussion of Isaiah 40:3 and Qumran intertextuality, see Charlesworth, "Intertextuality: Isaiah 40:3 and the Serek Ha-Yahad," in *The Quest for Context and Meaning: Studies in Biblical Intertextuality in Honor of James A. Sanders*, C. A.

"in the wilderness (ἐν τῇ ἐρήμῳ)" to prepare "the way of the Lord"—which was intended to mean the way for Jesus (see also Matt 3:3, Luke 3:4, and John 1:23).

The same verse was chosen and it, Isa 40:3, was interpreted in a way that marks the Qumranites and John the Baptizer as unique exegetes in the history of biblical interpretation. Each claimed that they were in the wilderness because they had heard the Voice. It had called them to prepare the Way of Yahweh. Each interpreted Isa 40:3 to mean: "A Voice is calling, 'In the wilderness prepare the Way of Yahweh.'"

J. E. Taylor cites Isa 40:3 as a possible link between John the Baptizer and the Qumran Essenes. She, however, misses the meaning each—probably not independently— gave to their unique interpretation of this verse. She dismisses any possible similarity with the claim that "Only if the interpretation is precisely the same can we suppose that the two may have been linked."[8] That is amazing; this type of rigid reasoning would demolish the basis for a *Synopsis Quattuor Evangeliorum* and the redactional analysis of the authors of Luke and Matthew in light of Mark, one of their sources, which they frequently change. Surely the fact that Matthew and Luke change Mark and do not quote from it "precisely," and interpret it differently, does not suggest they are not dependent upon, or influenced by, Mark. John the Baptizer, if he had left Qumran, would be free to interpret Isaiah in a way that was not "precisely the same." Yet, he would still be dependent on the Qumranites for the importance of the verse; moreover, in many ways, his interpretation of Isa 40:3 is virtually indistinguishable from Qumran.

John the Baptizer does interpret Isa 40:3 in ways remarkably similar to the Qumran Essenes. He and they

Evans and S. Talmon, eds. (Leiden, New York: Brill, 1997) pp. 197–224.

8   J. E. Taylor, *The Immerser: John the Baptist Within Second Temple Judaism* (Grand Rapids: Eerdmans, 1997) p. 25.

are in the wilderness to prepare the Way of Yahweh. Whereas other Jews then and now interpret this verse to mean that the Voice is in the wilderness calling the faithful, the Qumranites and John the Baptizer thought the Voice was calling them to prepare *in the wilderness* the Way of the Lord. This they believed and this they experienced. That is why the Qumranites in the wilderness dedicated all their energies towards the coming of Yahweh. That is why John the Baptizer chose to live in the wilderness and to proclaim the coming of the Lord. This parallel is significant enough in itself to suggest some unique and significant relationship between the Qumran Essenes and John the Baptizer.

Second, archaeological excavations at Qumran unearthed vast and numerous cisterns and *miqwaot* for water. The *Rule of the Community* and other compositions that were probably either composed at Qumran or obtained their final editing at Qumran stress the importance of water. It was necessary for purification. The initiate to Qumran Essenism took two years, at least, to pass the barriers erected around the *yaḥad* or Community. After passing all tests, the "Sons of the Dawn" could be admitted into the waters of impurity and then partake of the Meal of the Many. John the Baptizer, who is often called John the Baptist, was known by his occupation. He was the Baptizer. His mission was defined by baptism.

There is more. Like the Qumran Essenes, John the Baptizer connected his use of ritual lustration with a paradigmatic importance: Only those who had repented and cleansed their souls could receive ritualistic immersion.[9] Josephus reported that John did not teach that baptism was for repentance; rather, he demanded a necessary prerequisite for baptism—leading righteous lives, practicing justice towards others and God (*Ant* 18.117). These prerequisites for baptism are also found in the *Rule of the*

---

9   See esp. K. Berger, *The Truth Under Lock and Key? Jesus and the Dead Sea Scrolls,* translated by J. S. Currie (Louisville: Westminster/John Knox, 1995) pp. 57–58.

Community. Only those who had become purified morally and intellectually could enter into the *miqwaot* and cleansing cisterns; note 1QS 5.13–14 "He must not enter the water in order to touch the purity of the men of holiness. For they cannot be cleansed unless they turn away from their wickedness . . ." Both John and the Essenes claimed that only those who were leading righteous lives and then were subsequently cleansed by water were members of the faithful group that was prepared for the final acts of God, the coming judgment, and punishment of the wicked.

Third, the Qumran Essenes and John the Baptizer lived and worked in the same geographical location and they shared the same time. He worked only a few miles from Qumran. Recently, we have learned from the James Strange ostracon, discovered in the winter of 1996, that Essenes may have lived in Jericho or had associates in or near that ancient town. Thus, it seems that John the Baptizer lived and worked in the areas in which the Essenes were active and in which their main religious center was located. Surely, one should be open to the possibility that John the Baptizer at least knew about this devout sect of Jews.

Fourth, like the Qumranites, John's teaching was not only eschatological, but also apocalyptic. They shared the same fervor. Each stressed that the end of time is now. Other groups of Jews, of course, shared this perspective. But the Qumranites and John seemed to take it to extremes. It is one thing to think that the present is eschatological and apocalyptic; it is another to make it your focal point and almost only emphasis.

Fifth, both the Qumranites and John stressed that the present was the time of impending judgment. Both coupled this claim with a severe hatred for the wicked. At Qumran, the yearly ritual of entering the new covenant demanded cursing all "the Sons of Darkness." John is known for his fire-and-brimstone preaching: "He said to the crowds that came out to be baptized by him, "You brood of vipers! Who warned you to flee from the wrath to come? . . . Even now the ax is laid to the root of the trees; every tree therefore that does not bear good fruit is cut down and thrown into the fire" (Luke 3:7–9, cf. Matt 3:7–10).

Sixth, if Luke is correct, John the Baptizer was born into a priestly family that had significant duties in the Temple (Luke 1:5–25, 57–80). The Qumran Community obviously began as a group of priests who left or were expelled from the Temple sometime shortly after 150 BCE. In fact, the Dead Sea Scrolls make it abundantly clear that the Qumranites claimed to be the only legitimate high priests. They called themselves "the Sons of Aaron" and "the Sons of Zadok." The difference is slight since Zadok was a descendant of Aaron.

Seventh, Luke reports that John the Baptizer was "in the wilderness" before he began his preaching (Luke 1:80). Where would he have lived? How would he have survived? Some scholars rightly conclude that he may have lived for some time at Qumran. Josephus and others report that the Essenes habitually adopted young boys to train (*War* 2.8.2 paragraph 120). Perhaps John did spend his youth with the Qumranites. Josephus's time with Banas comes to mind, and he also was from a family of distinguished priests. We will never be certain, but speculation and some imagination is essential in any reconstruction of the past.

Eighth, according to Luke, within the crowds who came to John were tax collectors and soldiers (Luke 3:10–14). The crowds asked him what they should do after they had been baptized. He told them they needed only one garment and to give the others to the needy. He also told them to share their food with others. This injunction sounds remarkably like Qumran Essenism and John's own lifestyle.

Dissimilarities

Any search for meaning needs to amass all data. Not only similarities but also dissimilarities are essential for insight and reconstruction. The Qumranites and John were also different.

First, John the Baptizer was not predeterministic as were the Qumran Essenes. They believed that at birth one was assigned a certain amount of light and a certain amount of darkness. According to the *Horoscopes* (viz. 4Q186) each human has nine parts. Each person has some light and also some darkness. Apparently the most wicked had eight parts of darkness and only one part of light. The most perfect had eight parts of light and one part of darkness. This teaching explains why, according to the dualism of 1QS 3.13 – 4.26, a Son of Light could be led into "the ways of darkness" by the "Angel of Darkness." John would have none of this teaching. If our sources are trustworthy, he called all Israel to repent and to be baptized.

Second, John apparently related to all Israel (Mark 1:5, Matt 3:5, Luke 3:3). He did not teach that the largest segment of humanity should be hated. This was an aspect of Qumran theology that he could not accept.

Third, unlike the Qumranites, John evidenced a missionary zeal. We have found no missionary document at Qumran. The conciliatory tone of 4QMMT is clear, but it is not a tract for conversion.[10] *More Works of the Torah* is an appeal by the Qumranites to the leading priests in Jerusalem. It is probably not a letter. In this tract, the Qumranites explain their own perception of the inviolable importance of the solar calendar and the only way to understand and interpret Torah. It is not a missionary tract. There were no missionaries at Qumran. The missionary and the great preacher of impending doom was John (Matt 3:12, Luke 3:17–18). He was the Amos of the New Testament period.

Fourth, John told his hearers to go back to their tasks (cf. Luke 3:10–14). This seems obvious. Unlike the Qumranites, he did not teach them to withdraw from society. He

---

10   See esp. E. Qimron and J. Strugnell, et al., DJD 5; and J. Kampen and M. J. Bernstein, eds., *Reading 4QMMT: New Perspectives on Qumran Law and History*, SBL Symposium Series 2 (Atlanta: Scholars, 1996).

did not accept the high barriers of separation established by the Essenes, especially the Qumranite Essenes.

Fifth, John worked beside and in the Jordan. He did not work at Qumran. There is no explicit evidence in traditions about John in the New Testament or Josephus nor any hint in the Dead Sea Scrolls that the Baptizer was ever at Qumran.

Sixth, John was an isolated individual. He was sociologically unlike the Qumran *yaḥad* or Community in which all was shared collectively. At Qumran, meaning was obtained in oneness and in togetherness. These points make it clear that John was not a Qumran Essene.

Explaining these Similarities and Dissimilarities

How do we synthesize these points? What, then, is the relation of John the Baptizer to the Qumran Essenes? In *The Dead Sea Scrolls Today*, James C. VanderKam rightly points out that John is "an especially fitting candidate for possible contacts with Qumran" and "much in the New Testament picture of John reminds us of the Qumran Community and texts."[11] VanderKam wisely concludes that if John the Baptizer "ever was a member of the Qumran Community or visited the site, he must have later separated from it to pursue his independent, solitary ministry."[12] This is fair enough, but why? Why would he have joined it and then left it?

I found a possible answer when I was preparing the critical texts and translations of the copies of the *Rule of the Community*. This document is invaluable because it helps us see into the Community and hear the Qumran Essenes explain for themselves, certainly not for us, the rules and regulations of their Community. The central focus for our present concerns is the rules for the yearly renewal of the new covenant. The priests and Levites enter in order and

11   J. C. VanderKam, *The Dead Sea Scrolls Today* (Grand Rapids: Eerdmans, 1994) pp. 168, 169.
12   Ibid, p. 170.

each member of the Community must say aloud "Amen, amen" when chants are completed. It is easy to perceive that John would have said these words when the righteous were celebrated or the wicked cursed. But, there is one chant and malediction that would have become hard to repeat and eventually would be an anathema to him. The curse on others which includes the following words, "May God not be compassionate unto you when you cry out" (1QS 2.8) would have been difficult for John to support in light of his understanding of the God of forgiveness found throughout the Tanakh (or Old Testament) and especially in Psalm 51. John simply could not support such a curse as we find in the *Rule of the Community* with an "Amen, amen." He may have been drawn to the Community because it claimed to be "the community of truth, of virtuous humility, of merciful love," but he would have found that those attributes were reserved for the Community (1QS 2.23–25). The curses on those who left the Community or were expelled from it in 1QS 10–18 were filled with hatred, but some of those may well have been John's close friends. We have seen a possible reason why John the Baptizer would have left the Community if he had been a member of it.

That he had been a member seems probable because of the food he ate and the clothes he wore. If he had made the oaths required by members of the Community, he could not receive anything from one who was not an Essene. It was forbidden to give anything to one who had left or been expelled from the Community (1QS). Josephus describes the wretched life of those who kept their vows and died or nearly died from starvation until they were taken back again into the *yaḥad* or Community (*War*). So, we see John portrayed eating only locusts and wild honey and wearing animal skins. Why did he not accept food from those who came by the hundreds to be baptized by him? Why did he not accept clothing from others? Is it because he had promised God that he would keep his vows made in the Community?

However we answer these questions, they transport us back into the turmoil of first-century Judaism. There were more than a dozen groups and subgroups in first-century Judaism. In the end, John the Baptizer cannot and should not be portrayed as an Essene or one completely influenced by Essene theology. He was unique and he attracted disciples. One of them was called Jesus.

Jesus

These reflections have led us to consider Jesus. According to the Synoptic Gospels (Matthew, Mark, and Luke), Jesus came to John the Baptizer to be baptized by him. Mark explains in detail how Jesus was baptized in the Jordan by John. According to the Fourth Evangelist, Jesus was with John for a long period, leading a baptist movement himself. The Fourth Evangelist even reports that Jesus baptized in the land of Judea (3:22) and baptized more "disciples" than John the Baptizer.[13] According to Luke, Jesus and John the Baptizer were related. What, then, are the similarities between Jesus and the Essenes, especially the non-Qumran Essenes; that is, the Essenes living in Jerusalem and throughout Galilee?

At the outset, we must eliminate for comparison all traditions and texts that are shared by Jesus and the Essenes. Hence, we cannot discern if Jesus inherited any of the pictorial imagery so typical of his parables from the *Thanksgiving Hymns*. Most of this imagery and symbolism is found in

13 According to the Gospel of John, in 4:2, Jesus did not baptize but only his disciples. Yet, 4:1 states that "Jesus was making and baptizing more disciples than John . . . ." I am persuaded that 4:2 is a later addition to the Gospel to separate Jesus from John because of the followers of John who thought he, and not Jesus, was the Messiah, because the greater one always baptizes one who is lesser. The same phenomenon is seen in the history of the Synoptic tradition. Only Mark has John baptize Jesus. Matthew and Luke try to remove John the Baptizer from the picture.

the Tanakh (Old Testament) and in the Jewish apocryphal books. Second, we cannot discern links between Jesus' concept of a remnant and God's planting, so richly developed in the Dead Sea Scrolls, because this imagery is also found and developed in the Tanakh (Old Testament) and elsewhere. Jesus' monotheism derives from the Tanakh (Old Testament) and not from Qumran.

Jesus and the Essenes were both influenced by apocalypticism and messianism.[14] These ideas must also be eliminated for consideration. Seeking to discern any possible influence of the Essenes on Jesus at this point would ignore the obvious: apocalypticism and messianism, for example, are found in the *Psalms of Solomon* which was the hymnbook of a group of Jews living in Jerusalem at that time and similar in some ways to a group we call the Pharisees. Apocalypticism is developed in many Jewish documents, especially the *Books of Enoch*. This is a collection of at least five books that date from roughly 250 BCE to about the time of Herod the Great.[15] Many symbolic ideas and theological insights were inherited independently by Jesus and the Essenes from shared scriptures, especially Isaiah, Jeremiah, Ezekiel, and the Psalms.

14   For bibliographical references, see the detailed studies I
     have published on John the Baptizer and Jesus of Nazareth.
     Two recent books are especially helpful: J. J. Collins,
     Apocalypticism in the Dead Sea Scrolls (London and New
     York: Routedge, 1997) and C. A. Evans and P. W. Flint,
     eds., *Eschatology, Messianism, and the Dead Sea Scrolls*, Studies in the Dead Sea Scrolls and Related Literature 1(Grand
     Rapids: Eerdmans, 1997).
15   I have become persuaded that the *Parables of Enoch* (chapters 37–71 of 1En) date from approximately 37 to 4 BCE
     since they sociologically reflect the crises of landlessness
     typical of Herod's reign.

Striking Similarities and Links between Jesus and the Uniqueness of Qumran

What then might reveal some link between Jesus and the Essenes? First, both he and they lived and taught in the same location and at the same time. It is possible that Jesus met Essenes. The similarities will be listed in a random order of possible influence of Essene theology on Jesus.

Second, the possibility of some relation is increased when one recognizes that both Jesus and the Essenes shared *similar eschatological emphasis*. Scholars used to conclude that the Essenes had a futuristic eschatology and Jesus a realizing one. That misrepresents much of the Essene writings and also many of the sayings attributed to Jesus. Both the Essenes and Jesus taught and believed that the present is pregnant with the eschaton; that is to say, the future age is being experienced in the present age. The passages are too well known to repeat here. Eschatology was certainly in the air, and even apocalyptic eschatology as we know from such non-Qumran documents as the *Books of Enoch*. Thus, it is not clear how and in what ways, if at all, Jesus was influenced by some of the unique eschatological and apocalyptic ideas found in the Dead Sea Scrolls. That they shared this perspective is clear and would increase the chances of a basis for discussion with agreements and disagreements.

Third, both the Essenes and Jesus demanded *total dedication to God*. Only one thing was important: to dedicate all to preparing for God's day and God's imminent action. Jesus is reputed to have said that one who put his hand to the plow and looked backward was not worthy of the kingdom. Like the Essenes he taught that one must leave all behind, one's family, and one's possessions in the service of God. Such total dedication, which at times could undermine some of the commandments, forges the possibility of some significant relation between Jesus and the Essenes.

Fourth, like the Essenes, Jesus is characterized by *emphasizing the dawning day of judgment*. It is not possible to attribute this aspect of his teaching to the Essenes, since he may have inherited it from John the Baptizer. In that case, he may well have been indirectly influenced by the Essenes; that is, he could have been influenced by his teacher, John the Baptist, who may well have once been a Qumran Essene.

Fifth, like the Essenes, Jesus *devoted large sections of time to prayer*, and this dimension of his spirituality seems authentic even if the author of the Gospel of Luke develops it to punctuate his narrative. He most likely taught his followers a prayer which helped define them within the world of Early Judaism. One stichos of this prayer is usually translated "do not lead us into temptation." Some translators and commentators think the line means "do not lead us into testing" and then they add "which is too great for us." Support for this interpretative translation is found among the Dead Sea Scrolls. In the *Qumran Pseudepigraphic Psalms* we hear in a prayer that God "will test all" (4Q381 46 5) and that "his tested ones will praise him" (4Q381 24 6). The original language of the Lord's Prayer is Aramaic, in which the aphel means not only "cause us to enter" but also "allow us to enter." The latter avoids commentative additions and the translation of the Greek is improved by looking at the Syriac version, notably in Syrus Sinaiticus. It should be translated "do not allow us to enter into temptation." This perception is now found in the Qumran *Psalms Scroll*, edited by J. A. Sanders:

> Remember me and forget me not,
> And do not allow me to enter into
> situations too hard for me. (Ps 155:11)[16]

Sixth, Jesus' primary teaching concerns *the Rule of God* (or Kingdom of God) which he depicted sometimes as futuristic and at other times virtually present (especially in his

---

16   See Charlesworth, "The *Beth Essentiae* and the Permissive Meaning of the Hiphil (Aphel)," in *Of Scribes and Scrolls [John Strugnell Festschrift]*, ed. H. W. Attridge, J. J. Collins, and T. H. Toblin, S.J. (New York, London: Doubleday, 1990) pp. 67–78, esp. see p. 77.

parables). The Essenes also depicted God as king and knew about the extreme importance of his kingdom. The teaching is dominant in the *Angelic Liturgy* (or the *Songs of the Sabbath Sacrifices*). Note these passages: "For in the splendor of praise is the glory of his kingdom (מלכותו)" (4Q403 li 32); ". . . and he will bless all who are app[ointed for] righteous[ness, who pr]aise his glorious kingdom [. . .] forever, with seven [wondrous] wo[rds, to be for] eternal peace" (4Q403 l 25–26). God is not called Yahweh; he is "the king of the angels (מלך מלאכים)."[17] It is certainly conceivable, perhaps probable, that Jesus' teaching on the kingship of God and his kingdom was influenced, in some still undetermined ways, by Essenes.

Seventh, somewhat like the Essenes, especially those at Qumran, *Jesus redefined the family*. It consisted of those in the spiritual group. The social oneness of the *yaḥad*, the Community, is similar to Jesus' declaration that not his mother and brothers are his family but those who have left all for the kingdom (Mark 3:34–35, Matt 12:49–50, Luke 8:21).

Eighth, at Qumran a *unique interpretation of scripture* was practiced. It is the famous *pesher* interpretation of Torah. It was both eschatological and pneumatic; that is, the prophecies in scripture pertained only to the present time of the Community—the Endtime—and they can be understood only through the presence of the Holy Spirit and the mysteries vouchsafed only to the Righteous Teacher (1QpHab 7). Jesus' interpretation of Torah was sometimes markedly similar to this *pesher* method. According to Luke, Jesus "full of the Holy Spirit" (4:1) returned from being "in the wilderness" (4:2) to teach in the synagogues of Galilee. He entered Nazareth, opened the scroll of Isaiah on Shabbat, and read from 61 and 58. Then, in something like Qumran fashion, he sat down and announced "Today (σήμερον) this scripture has been fulfilled (πεπλήρωται) in your hearing" (4:21).

17   Masada ShirShabb ii 7; cf. 4Q403 1 i 1.

Ninth, Jesus honors those who have made themselves eunuchs for "the sake of the kingdom of heaven" (Matt 19:12). Who could he be referring to? It must denote a group of men who were *celibate*. If so, the most likely candidates would be the Essenes, since Philo, Josephus, and Pliny the Elder all report that the Essenes, or some of them, were celibate.[18]

Tenth, Jesus uses the word coined by the Essenes for themselves: "Sons of Light." As David Flusser, in his recent *Jesus* and elsewhere, points out, this technical term "Sons of Light" is unique to the Essenes and to literature influenced by them.[19] Both Luke and John report that Jesus used the *terminus technicus* "Sons of Light." If he did, and if this term was used by the Essenes and referred only to them, then it follows that Jesus knew and was influenced by the Essenes. Whether he spoke approvingly or disapprovingly about them is not our present concern. That he used their term is evidence of influence.

Eleventh, the concept of the Holy Spirit as a separate and hypostatic being is found first in the Qumran Scrolls. There in the wilderness, the followers of the Righteous Teacher felt the presence of "the Holy Spirit" as they had earlier officiating in the Temple. Hence, they obtained a powerful basis for the *raison d'etre* for being in the wilderness to prepare the way for Yahweh according to Isa 40:3. The Holy Spirit was with them and thus they lived in "the House of Holiness" and could be certain they were none other than "the Holy Ones" and the "Most Holy of Holy Ones." Even angels were experienced as present with them in the בית קודש ("the House of Holiness") which was "holy" because the רוח קודש ("the Holy Spirit") was present enabling them to consider themselves קדשים ("the Holy Ones"), and קודש קודשים ("the Most Holy Ones"),

---

18   Philo (*Hypothetica* 11.14 par. 380), Josephus (*War* 2.8.2 par. 120) and Pliny the Elder (*Nat. Hist.* 5.17.4).

19   D. Flusser, *Jesus* (Jerusalem, 1997) also see Flusser, *Judaism and the Origins of Christianity* (Jerusalem: Magnes, 1988).

and even קדושי קודש קודשים ("the Most Holy of Holy Ones"). It is clear that the Qumran Essenes developed the concept of holiness, the Holy Spirit, the House of Holiness, and the concept of being "the Holy Ones" in a way that is unique within early Jewish theology. When Jesus uses the word "the Holy Spirit," it may well suggest that he has been influenced by the Essenes.

Before we assess these eleven shared characteristics in the attempt to discern if Jesus was influenced in any way by Essenes, it is wise to keep a balanced approach to the vast amount of data to be digested and summarized. Thus, it is imperative to include a review of the ways Jesus was most definitely unlike the Essenes.

Polemic against the Essenes

Passages in the Gospels indicate that Jesus appears to be directing some of his teaching against emphases known to be typical of the Essenes. Six areas, in no distinct order, help clarify ways Jesus would have disagreed with Essenes.

First, the Essenes were *the writing sect* within Judaism. They have left us a library of their own compositions and many other early Jewish texts composed by other groups within Judaism as well as virtually all the books in the Tanakh (Old Testament). Jesus wrote nothing. The Essenes were authors. Jesus was an itinerant preacher, whom many considered a prophet with oracles.

Second, more than any Jewish sect or group, the Essenes elevated the requirements for observing *the Sabbath*. Jesus also observed the Sabbath; he never broke the Sabbath regulations found in the Tanakh (Old Testament). But, according to the heightened Sabbath regulations of some Pharisees and the Essenes, he had broken their rules for the Sabbath. He simply did not accept their interpretations of Sabbath laws.

On one occasion, he seems to have deliberately rejected a teaching known to be typical, and perhaps unique, to the Essenes. He asked his hearers who would leave a sheep dying in a pit on the Sabbath (only in Matt and at 12:11). The question seems absurd. It makes sense only when we realize that the non-Qumran Essenes, represented by the *Damascus Document*, thought and taught that an animal which falls into a pit on the Sabbath must not be helped out of the pit (CD 11:13). They reasoned that such a task would constitute working on the Sabbath. I am persuaded that Jesus seems to be directing his thoughts specifically against Essenes and their teaching. Assuming that this is so turns an otherwise absurd saying of Jesus into a meaningful text within a now disclosed context.

Third, the Essenes, perhaps more than the Pharisees and Sadducees, emphasized *ritual cleanliness*. Josephus reports that the concern for purity within the group necessitated ritual cleansing if a lower Essene touched a more advanced Essene. Jesus dispatched many of this teachings against the increasing demands for purity in his society, and some may have been directed against the Essenes. Jesus, in contrast to them, taught that it is not what enters the humans that defiles them. It is what comes out of them (Mark 7:14–23, Matt 15:10–20). This was certainly a revolutionary teaching within Judaism; it was courageous and perhaps led to his suffering and eventual transference from some priests to Pilate.

Fourth, the Essenes taught *supreme loyalty to God and also to a priestly tradition*. Jesus, in contrast, taught utter loyalty to God alone. According to a fragment of the *Damascus Document* found in Cave 4, a person with scabs on the scalp must cut his hair so that the priest may count the number of hairs that have grown back. By this process, the priest could announce what caused the illness. Perhaps speaking directly against this teaching which would attract public attention, Jesus stated that the very hairs of our head are *numbered by God* (Matt 10:30, Luke 12:7).[20] He meant to

---

20   I have published this analysis in Greek; see "The Dead Sea Scrolls and the Saying of Jesus 'But the hairs of your head all are numbered,'" in *Bulletin of Biblical Studies* 16 (1997) 11–26.

stress that God is concerned about the welfare of each of us. This saying of Jesus has lain without meaning in the Gospels for about two thousand years. Now, we can understand it. Jesus is stating that our source of loyalty and dedication is not to a priest but to God. I am convinced that Jesus may well have known and spoken against this Essene practice.

Fifth, the Essenes were *deterministic*, as we noted in summarizing the possible links between John the Baptizer and the Essenes. Jesus would have recoiled against the Essene teaching that some humans are damned at birth. He taught that all humans are children of God—perhaps he meant only Jews, but he did not consign some Jews, and the majority of them, to darkness. Was he reacting against the teaching of the Essenes? Unfortunately, our sources are too selected to be of much help in pursuing this issue further.

Sixth, following from the preceding point, it is clear that the Essenes were the *most exclusivistic group within Judaism*. Jesus was a missionary prophet declaring God's good news to all his hearers. The Essenes and he stood at opposite ends of the spectrum of answers to the question, Who is my neighbor? The Essenes answer was that the neighbor is only a fellow Son of Light. Jesus had a paradigmatically different answer. He taught that even the Samaritan, who was despised by many Jews, is our neighbor (Luke 10:25–37).

Seventh, the Essenes taught *love* only for a fellow Son of Light and institutionalized hatred for all Sons of Darkness—all who were not in their elect group (1QS 1–2). Jesus taught love, and his teaching was unlimited, as we know from his new commandment found only in the Gospel of John (13:34), the supreme poem on love written by Paul in 1 Corinthians 13, and the teachings in the Synoptics that stress that we must love even our enemies (Matt 5:44). Here Jesus' teaching is so contrasted with the Essenes that one is left to ponder if he was directing his teaching, at times, against Essenes.

Was Jesus an Essene or Anti-Essene?

These eleven similarities and seven dissimilarities leave us with many issues to ponder. On the one hand, we must avoid the conclusion that Jesus was in no way influenced by Essenes. To claim that he was unique and not influenced by his contemporaries may indicate the intrusion of Christian dogmatics. On the other hand, to claim that he was significantly influenced by the Essenes is not sufficiently supported by the ancient sources.

The eleven similarities are helpful. The first five lead to the possibility that Jesus conversed with Essenes and shared some of their ideas and general perspective, at least on some major points. Similarities six through eleven lead to the possibility that Jesus was most likely influenced by Essene teachings on God as king and his kingdom, the importance of oneness within the sect, the *pesher* method of interpreting Scripture, and the importance of full dedication to God as illustrated by the saying about eunuchs who live for the kingdom. If Jesus used the *terminus technichus* "Sons of Light" and if it is a sign of Essene influence, then he was definitely referring to Essenes when he used that term. Likewise, if the Essene concept of the Holy Spirit was used by Jesus, then he was certainly influenced by their theology, at least with this term.

The seven points in which Jesus seems to be refuting Essene teachings tend to make a much stronger case of Jesus' knowledge of Essenes. He does seem to engage them at crucial points in which he differs from them. The particulars, especially the teaching about helping an animal out of a pit on the Sabbath and God counting the hairs on our head, tend to clinch the argument for me that Jesus intermittently polemized against Essenes.

For others, the evidence is suggestive, but not conclusive. All should study the evidence carefully and come to their own understanding.[21] Virtually no distinguished scholar has concluded that Jesus was an Essene, although there are too many self-acclaimed scholars who have tried to convince the masses of this conclusion. Some specialists do conclude that Jesus was anti-Essene. Foremost among them would be Y. Yadin.[22] The primary sources and the significant similarities and dissimilarities lead me to conclude that Jesus should not be simply categorized as an Essene or anti-Essene. Some of his teachings are clearly, in my viewpoint, anti-Essene but others seem to agree with them. In summation, Jesus most likely conversed with the Essenes and came away admiring their dedication to God as king, their apocalyptic and eschatological fervor, and their perception of the present as the age of the fulfillment of prophecies and the time of judgment. In the end, he had to part company with them because of their dualistic determinism, their concept of purity, and their exclusiveness. Jesus was no more an Essene than he was a Hillelite Pharisee.

Conclusion

Fifty years is a jubilee. Fifty years ago, the Dead Sea Scrolls were seen again by human eyes after almost two thousand years. The insights and ideas obtained from these Jewish documents are bequeathed to us directly and not via the media of Christian scribes, as is so often the case with the Old Testament Pseudepigrapha and other early Jewish documents. The new perspectives and data help us reconstruct the world of Second Temple Judaism, especially

21   For a detailed analysis of John the Baptizer and the Essenes, see Charlesworth's contribution in the BYU Dead Sea Scrolls volume edited by D. Parry, et al. (in press). For the analysis of the ways Jesus may have been influenced by Essenes, see esp. Charlesworth, *Jesus and the Dead Sea Scrolls* (New York: Doubleday, 1995).

22   Y. Yadin, *The Temple Scroll: The Hidden Law of the Dead Sea Sect* (London: Thames and Hudson, 1985) p. 241, "I am convinced that Jesus was anti-Essene . . ."

during the time that another sect was taking shape: the Palestinian Jesus Movement.[23]

We can now speculate, with significant support, that John the Baptizer was most likely once related in some way to the Essene group at Qumran. Prior to his ministry of baptizing in the Jordan near Jericho, he may well have been a member of the Qumran Community. If so, we can understand why he stressed Isaiah, interpreted 40:3 as did the Qumran Essenes, and refused to accept food or clothing from other Jews.

New Testament scholars, sometimes somewhat grudgingly, are admitting that archaeology is important and that the Dead Sea Scrolls and related documents help us understand the context of a New Testament text. Jesus' message must be understood in terms of his original audience, which most likely included not only the large number of Am Ha-aretz, Pharisees, Samaritans, and Enoch groups, but also Essenes. He seems to have known some of their unique teachings. There are significant reasons to resist the fallacy of declaring Jesus to be an Essene; but there are also reasons to resist portraying him as anti-Essene. Jesus was similar to the Essenes in stressing eschatological and apocalyptic Jewish theology, in employing the concept of the Holy Spirit, in focusing his message on the Kingdom of God (better, Rule of God), and in announcing the impending judgment. He was also similar to the Pharisees, namely Hillel, especially in seeing the core of Hebrew Scriptures as portrayed in the first two Mosaic commandments, but also in affirming the moral theology of the Golden Rule (if Hillel and Jesus did say what is attributed to them).[24] Nvertheless, Jesus does not belong within any one of the

23 See O. Betz and R. Riesner, "Did the Essenes Turn to Jesus as Messiah?" in *Jesus, Qumran, and the Vatican* (New York: Crossroad, 1994) pp. 141–56.
24 See Charlesworth and L. L. Johns, eds., *Hillel and Jesus* (Minneapolis: Fortress, 1997).

groups or sects within Early Judaism. He was unique in numerous ways and his synthesis of Jewish ideas belonged solely to him. Jesus spoke directly, simply, and by citing only the authority of Torah and God.

Without any doubt, the only way to understanding John the Baptizer and Jesus is through archaeology and the literary sources that help us understand and reconstruct the world of pre-70 Palestinian Judaism. On the one hand, this fact is pellucidly clear when we hear the self-proclaimed prophets of today, such as David Koresh, who ignore all sources except an English Bible and subjectivity. On the other hand, the fact becomes palpable when one holds a leather scroll once held and considered Scripture or full of God's revelation by Jews who lived in ancient Palestine before the destruction of Jerusalem in 70 CE. Pride of place in all these endeavors must go to the hundreds of scrolls hidden in caves south of Jericho in the spring of 68—that is, the so-called Dead Sea Scrolls.

John the Baptizer and his erstwhile student, Jesus of Nazareth, are appearing as men of flesh and blood within a social context, thanks to these ancient Jewish compositions hid for two millennia in desert caves. Ancient data and archeological realia invite modern individuals to explore that time and place when the values and dreams of western culture were taking definite shape. The Righteous Teacher and his disciples seem to have influenced John the Baptizer. He influenced Jesus.

I remember as a teenager standing beside the everglades. I would toss a pebble into a placid pond and marvel at the ripples. Something like that can still be seen and felt today as we think about the Dead Sea Scrolls and the meaning of life and history. After fifty years of research, scholars have helped us grasp more accurately how modern Judaism and the Palestinian Jesus Movement began. Like Newton, we Dead Sea Scrolls experts sometimes feel like the child in our past, running in and out among the waves, stopping momentarily to pick up tiny sea shells.

Epilogue

Why do archaeologists rise long before dawn to scamper into a five-meter square in which they will crawl in the debris of ancients? What motivates them? Why do Qumran experts slave over tiny fragments in the attempt to assemble the world's most excruciatingly demanding jigsaw puzzle—in fact, over six hundred puzzling documents, 90 percent missing, and all mixed together? Why have so many sacrificed so much? What is the driving force? Perhaps T. S. Eliot came close to articulating what we feel:

> We shall not cease from exploration
> And the end of all our exploring
> Will be to arrive where we started
> And know the place for the first time.

I have seen that thought silently shining in eyes as one captivated by the meaning of a balk momentarily glanced my way. Time often writes poetry in refuse as archaeologists translate realia. Foul-smelling leather scrolls breathe secrets from spiritual ancestors.

Paul and the Dead Sea Scrolls

James D. G. Dunn

The influence of the Dead Sea Scrolls on Pauline studies falls quite neatly into two main periods: the impact of the earlier published scrolls and the impact of those more recently published.

I

The earlier phase is well illustrated in two collections—the one edited by Krister Stendahl,[1] and the other by Jerome Murphy-O'Connor[2]—and is well documented by Herbert Braun's review.[3] The early soundings made by David Flusser succeeded in identifying several of the reefs which

1   *The Scrolls and the New Testament* (New York: Harper & Row, 1957). I cite the UK edition (London: SCM, 1958).

2   *Paul and Qumran: Studies in New Testament Exegesis* (London: Chapman, 1968); reissued with a new Foreword by J. H. Charlesworth, as *Paul and the Dead Sea Scrolls* (New York: Crossroad, 1990).

3   *Qumran und das Neue Testament*, 2 vols. (Tübingen: Mohr-Siebeck, 1966). See also the more recent summary by

connected the two thought worlds below the surface.[4] In this first phase, then, a number of features within the principal scrolls were noted which shed illuminating light on Paul's letters, both major motifs and individual passages. In almost every case, it is not a matter of direct dependence, but of the scrolls illuminating the religious and theological context from within which Paul came and which is strongly reflected in his own writing.[5] The most commonly highlighted were as follows.

Human need and divine righteousness. An early point of contact was the recognition of a striking similarity between Paul's and Qumran's assessment of the human condition. Much quoted has been 1QH 12(formerly 4).29–30:[6]

> What is a creature of clay for such marvels to be done,
> whereas he is in iniquity from the womb
> and in guilty unfaithfulness until his old age?
> Righteousness, I know, is not of man
> nor is perfection of way of the son of man.

Immediate comparison with a key Pauline text like Rom 3:20–26 is obviously invited.[7]

H.-W. Kuhn, "The Impact of the Scrolls on the Understanding of Paul," in D. Dimant and U. Rappaport, eds., *The Dead Sea Scrolls: Forty Years of Research* (Leiden: Brill and Jerusalem: Magnes, 1992) pp. 327–39, which draws principally on Braun's review of parallels.

4   D. Flusser, "The Dead Sea Sect and Pre-Pauline Christianity," *ScriHin* 4 (1958) pp. 215–66, reprinted in his *Judaism and the Origins of Christianity* (Jerusalem: Magnes, 1988) pp. 23–74—missed by Braun.

5   We have space here only to point up the parallel features between Paul and the Dead Sea Scrolls; to analyze the differences between them, even on the points of parallel, is beyond the scope of the paper.

6   English translations are from G. Vermes, *The Complete Dead Sea Scrolls in English* (London: Allen/Penguin, 1997), unless otherwise stated.

7   Braun, *Qumran*, vol. 1, p. 173. The discussion as to whether Paul's spirit/flesh antithesis is the same as Qumran's

The parallel runs on into what has been regarded as the classic Pauline theology of justification by faith.[8] Here the most quoted text has been 1QS 11.9–15:

> As for me, I belong to wicked mankind,
> to the company of unjust flesh.
>
> For mankind has no way
> and man is unable to establish his steps
> since justification (מִשְׁפָּט) is with God
> and perfection of way is out of his hand.
>
> As for me, if I stumble, the mercies of God
> shall be my eternal salvation.
> If I stagger because of the sin of flesh, my justification
> (מִשׁפָטי) shall be by the righteousness of God
> (בצדקת אל) which endures for ever.
>
> He will draw me near by his grace,
> and by his mercy (חסד) will he bring my justification
> (מִשׁפָטי).
> He will judge me in the righteousness of his truth
> (בצדקת אמתו)
> and in the greatness of his goodness he will pardon all
> my sins.
> Through his righteousness (צדקה) he will cleanse me
> of the uncleanness of man
> and of the sins of the children of men.

spirit/spirit antithesis (see particularly K. G. Kuhn, "New Light on Temptation, Sin and Flesh in the New Testament," and W. D. Davies, "Paul and the Dead Sea Scrolls: Flesh and Spirit," both in Stendahl, *The Scrolls and the New Testament*, pp. 94–113 and pp. 157–82; Flusser, *ScrHie* 4, "The Dead Sea Sect and Pre-Pauline Christianity" pp. 60–71) does not affect the point here (see further below under "Dualism").

8   So, e.g., M. Burrows, *The Dead Sea Scrolls* (London: Secker & Warburg, 1955) p. 334; K. Stendahl, "The Scrolls and the New Testament: An Introduction and a Perspective," in Stendahl ed., *The Scrolls and the New Testament*, p. 9; M. Black, *The Scrolls and Christian Origins* (London: Nelson, 1961) pp. 125–26.

The closeness of the parallel is not to be denied, even if the translation of מִשְׁפָּט as "justification" is open to question,[9] since the understanding of צדקה as God's "saving righteousness" is precisely what Paul presupposes when he introduces this as his key concept in Rom 1:16–17.[10] The point of comparison is the confidence in God's righteousness, and that both expected this confidence to be justified in the final judgment (cf. Rom 2:12–16; 3:20; Gal 5:5). Yet, despite this text being brought into discussions of Paul's theology of justification at a fairly early stage,[11] the implications for a rethinking of why Paul's theology was so polemical at this point ("by faith and *not* by works of the law") were hardly followed up. If Qumran, notwithstanding its extreme nomism, retained such a powerful sense of dependence on divine חסד, צדקה, and אמת and such clear confidence in God's saving righteousness, to what was it in his ancestral religion that Paul seemed to be objecting so strongly?

Pneumatology and Eschatology

A passage which drew considerable early attention is the famous two spirits section of 1QS (3.13 – 4.26).[12] It seemed to provide several points of connection. For one thing, the

9   P. Benoit, "Qumran and the New Testament," in Murphy-O'Connor, *Paul and Qumran* pp. 26–27.

10   See also Kuhn, "Impact," pp. 332–23; cf. M. A. Seifrid, *Justification by Faith: The Origin and Development of a Central Pauline Theme*, NovTSup 68 (Leiden: Brill, 1992) pp. 103–6.

11   So particularly P. Stuhlmacher, *Gerechtigkeit Gottes bei Paulus*, FRLANT 87 (Göttingen: Vandenhoeck, 1965) pp. 154–55; K. Kertelge, *"Rechtfertigung" bei Paulus*, NtA 3 (Münster: Aschendorff, 1967) p. 29.

12   The lack of attestation of this passage in the a-j 4QS fragments (see documentation by Qimron and Charlesworth in J. H. Charlesworth, ed., *The Dead Sea Scrolls: Rule of the Community and Related Documents* [Tübingen: Mohr-Siebeck and Louisville: Westminster John Knox, 1994] pp. 55–56) was not, of course, initially appreciated. But, according to Qimron and Charlesworth, "probably 3.13 – 4.26 (or at

idea of an eschatological cleansing by the Spirit seemed common to both Paul and Qumran (1QS 3.6–8; 4.21; cf. 1 Cor 6:11; 12:13).[13] The sense that this had already happened for the Qumran psalmist, that the Spirit was a present experience, is as clear in 1QH 4(formerly 17).17 and 26 and 15(formerly 7).6–7 as in such Pauline texts (cf. also e.g., 1 Cor 2:12; Gal 4:6; 1 Thess 4:8).[14] More prominent elsewhere is the sense of realizing eschatology (particularly in the Habakkuk *pesher*) and the claim to be already participating in "the new covenant" (CD 6.19; 8.21; 19.33–34), which can be readily paralleled with such Pauline texts as Gal 4:4–5 and 2 Cor 3:6.[15] More striking still is the parallel

least sections of it) were known by heart by all members of the community"; and they hazard the guess that "perhaps 3.13 – 4.14 derives directly from his [the Righteous Teacher's] teachings" (*Rule of the Community*, vol. 1, p. 3).

13 Flusser, "The Dead Sea Sect and Pre-Pauline Christianity" 54–60; Braun, *Qumran*, vol. 1, pp. 175–76. 1QS 3.6–8—"It is through the spirit of true counsel . . . that all his sins shall be expiated . . . He shall be cleansed from all his sins by the spirit of holiness . . ."; 1QS 4.21—"He will cleanse him of all wicked deeds with the spirit of holiness; like purifying waters he will shed upon him the spirit of truth . . . And he shall be plunged into the spirit of purification"; 1 Cor 6.11—"you were washed . . . in the Spirit of our God"; 1 Cor 12:13—"in one Spirit we were all baptized into one body . . . and were all watered with the one Spirit."

14 Braun, *Qumran*, vol. 1, pp. 179–81, 189, 210. 1QH 4.17—"[I give thee thanks] because of the spirits which thou hast given to me"; 4.26—"[I thank thee, O Lord, for] thou didst shed [thy] Holy Spirit upon thy servant." 1 Cor 2:12—"We have received not the spirit of the world, but the Spirit which is from God"; Gal 4:6—"God sent the Spirit of his Son into our hearts"; 1 Thess 4:8—"God who gives his Holy Spirit to us."

15 Braun, *Qumran*, vol. 1, pp. 180, 198–89, 211–12; vol. 2, pp. 281–83.

between 1QS 3.13 – 4.26 and Rom 7:7–25,[16] with the common sense of the individual divided, or torn in two, between good and bad, caught in what we might in each case describe as the eschatological tension between two cosmic potentialities, between the already and the not yet.[17] The parallel is not to be undermined by denying a sense of the already to Qumran, as though they could only reach forward towards something which Paul already enjoyed,[18] since the argument underplays both the sense of a decisive "already" in the Dead Sea Scrolls and the equal sense of a "not yet" in Paul.[19]

Dualism and Predestination

In the 1QS 3–4 passage, the eschatology takes on a strongly dualistic note in the talk of the two "spirits of truth and falsehood," "the spirits of light and darkness" (1QS 3.19, 25; 4.23).[20] Here, too, we may compare Paul's readiness to

16   1QS 4.15–17, 23–24—"The nature of all the children of men is ruled by these (two spirits), and during their life all the hosts of men have a portion of their divisions and walk in (both) their ways . . . For God has established the spirits in equal measure until the final age, and has set everlasting hatred between their divisions . . . Until now the spirits of truth and injustice struggle in the hearts of men and they walk in both wisdom and folly . . ." Rom 7:22–23; 8:6—"I delight in the law of God in terms of the inner person, but I see another law in my members, warring against the law of my mind and taking me captive by the law of sin which is in my members . . . The mind-set of the flesh is death, but the mind-set of the Spirit is life and peace."

17   Braun, *Qumran*, vol. 1, pp. 177–79, referring particularly to his own "Römer 7.7–25 und das Selbstverständnis des Qumran-Frommen," *ZTK* 56 (1959) pp. 1–18.

18   Benoit, "Qumran and the New Testament," pp. 20–21.

19   See also H.-W. Kuhn, *Enderwartung und gegenwärtiges Heil: Untersuchungen zu den Gemeindeliedern von Qumran*, SUNT 4 (Göttingen: Vandenhoeck, 1966).

20   Braun, *Qumran*, vol. 2, pp. 172–74.

talk of two or more spirits in Christian experience—"a spirit of slavery" and "the spirit of adoption" (Rom 8:15), the need to discern between spirits (1 Cor 12:10), and the danger of being "zealous for spirits" (1 Cor 14:12)[21]—and his equal readiness to contrast those of the day with those of the night (Rom 13:12–13; 1 Thess 5:4–8; Eph 5:8–14).[22] That this dualism is also expressed in strongly predestinarian terms in the same two spirits passage (especially 1QS 3.15 – 4.1, 15–16, 25–26; also 1QM 13.9–14) should be no surprise to those familiar with Paul's teaching in the same letter to the Roman Christians (especially Rom 9:15–23).[23] The point is not that either set of writings offers an easy solution to the unresolved conflict between predestinarian teaching and the eschatological tension still experienced by members of the authorial group. The point is rather that both the Qumran covenanters and Paul bear surprisingly similar testimony to the same tension and the same theological dissonance. However divergent their theological rationale, phenomenologically speaking they are very close.

21   See further Braun, *Qumran*, vol. 2, pp. 258–61.
22   Braun, *Qumran*, vol. 1, pp. 185–86, 219–22; Kuhn, "The Impact of the Scrolls on the Understanding of Paul," pp. 328–89. I include Colossians and Ephesians within Pauline literature since they featured so much in the earlier comparisons between Paul and Qumran, although Ephesians in particular is usually regarded in Pauline scholarship as deutero-Pauline.
23   Flusser, "The Dead Sea Sect and Pre-Pauline Christianity" in *ScrHie* 4, pp. 28–32; Braun, *Qumran* 2.247–8; G. Maier, *Mensch und freier Wille nach den jüdischen Religionsparteien zwischen Ben Sira und Paulus*, WUNT 12 (Tübingen: Mohr-Siebeck, 1971). Charlesworth in the new foreword to Murphy-O'Connor, quotes Magen Broshi: "Perhaps the most important theological point differentiating the sectarians from the rest of Judaism was their belief in predestination, coupled with a dualistic view of the world" (*Paul and Qumran*, p. xiv).

Divine Revelation

Another feature of the scrolls which caught early attention was the prominence of the claim to have been given knowledge and insight into divine mysteries, a privilege given to and through the Righteous Teacher in particular. As the Habakkuk commentary explicitly states: "that he who reads may read it speedily" (Hab 2:2). Interpreted, this concerns the Righteous Teacher, to whom God made known all the mysteries of the words of his servants the prophets (1QpHab 7.3–5).

Or presumably in the Teacher's own words in the *Hymn Scroll*:

> These things I know
> by the wisdom which comes from thee,
> for thou hast unstopped my ears
> to marvelous mysteries (1QH 9[formerly 1].21).

> To the elect of righteousness
> Thou hast made me a banner,
> and a discerning interpreter of wonderful mysteries
>   (1QH 10[formerly 2].13).

> Through me Thou hast illumined
> the face of the congregation
> and hast shown thine infinite power.
> For thou hast given me knowledge
> through thy marvelous mysteries
>   (1QH 12[formerly 4].27).

Particularly fascinating have been the parallels with the later Pauline letters, Colossians and Ephesians, with their similar emphases on a "mystery" which had been revealed, particularly to and through Paul himself: "the commission which was given to me for you, to make the word of God fully known, the mystery which has been hidden from the ages and from the generations. But now it has been revealed to his saints" (Col 1:25–26); "the mystery was made known to me by revelation . . . in former generations this mystery was not made known to humankind, as it has now been revealed to his holy apostles and prophets" (Eph 3:3, 5).[24] Of course, these parallels are hardly exclusive to Paul and Qumran, but it was the prominence of this feature in the scrolls which brought home to Pauline scholars the influence of the earlier Danielic motif. It is also true that Qumran and Paul understood the "mysteries" (Qumran) or "mystery" (Paul) rather differently. But certainly, the sense of the divine purpose settled long before, attested in Scripture, but now unveiled by eschatological revelation and requiring a fundamental reshaping of identity is common to both Qumran and Paul.[25]

Temple and Sacrifice

One other area which caught early attention involved the parallels discerned between the Qumran Community's sense of itself as a priestly community, as in effect fulfilling the role of the Temple, and Paul's perception of the Christian churches. Flusser was one of the first to note the parallel in the thought of "spiritual" sacrifice at Qumran and the language of Rom 12:1—the function of sacrifice fulfilled in the one case by "prayer rightly offered" (1QS 9.4–5; CD 11.20–21, citing Prov 15:8), and in the other by "the offering up of your bodies as a living sacrifice" (Rom 12:1).[26]

24   This feature proved to be of particular interest for the contributors to the symposium edited by Murphy-O'Connor and Benoit, "Qumran and the New Testament" pp. 21–24; J. Coppens, "'Mystery' in the Theology of Saint Paul and its Parallels at Qumran," in Murphy-O'Connor, *Paul and Qumran* pp. 132–58; F. Mussner, "Contributions Made by Qumran to the Understanding of the Epistle to the Ephesians," *Paul and Qumran* particularly pp. 159–63. See also R. E. Brown, *The Semitic Background of the Term "Mystery" in the New Testament,* Facet Book (Philadelphia: Fortress, 1968).

25   See further, M. N. A. Bockmuehl, *Revelation and Mystery in Ancient Judaism and Pauline Christianity*, WUNT 2.36 (Tübingen: Mohr-Siebeck, 1990).

26   Flusser, in *ScrHie* 4, "The Dead Sea Sect and Pre-Pauline Christianity" pp. 40–42.

The first of the new Society for New Testament Monograph Series, by Bertil Gärtner, was devoted to a comparison between a concept of the "new temple" in Qumran (citing, inter alia, 1QS 5.5ff.; 8.4ff.; 9.3ff.; 4QFlor) and Pauline passages like 1 Cor 3:16–17 and Eph 2:18–22.[27] And subsequently, in the same series, Michael Newton extended the comparison to the concept of purity. Though the weight given to purity concerns is very different in each case, they are by no means unimportant for Paul, and the fact that he gives them the attention that he does can be elucidated by the centrality of such concerns at Qumran.[28]

Particular Texts

Finally, of individual texts we may instance four from the Pauline *Hauptbriefe* by way of illustration.

One parallel which naturally caught early attention was the use made of Hab 2:4 by both Qumran and Paul. "The righteous shall live by his faith" was interpreted by the Habakkuk *pesher* as concerning "all those who observe the law in the house of Judah, whom God will deliver from the house of judgment because of their suffering and because of their faith in the Righteous Teacher" (1QpHab 8.1–3). For Paul, however, it served as a crucial confirmatory text that justification is by faith, that is, by faith in Christ Jesus or, alternatively expressed, by faith in the God who raised Jesus from the dead (Rom 1:17, elaborated in 3:21 – 4:25; Gal 3:11, elaborated in 2:16 – 3:29).[29] It is also relevant to note in the

27	B. Gärtner, *The Temple and the Community in Qumran and the New Testament*, SNTSMS 1 (Cambridge: University Press, 1965). See also G. Klinzing, *Die Umdeutung des Kultus in der Qumrangemeinde und im Neuen Testament*, SUNT 7 (Göttingen: Vandenhoeck, 1971).

28	M. Newton, *The Concept of Purity at Qumran and in the Letters of Paul*, SNTSMS 53 (Cambridge: University Press, 1985).

29	"It would almost seem as if this (faith in Christ) were a Pauline polemic against the Midrash (1QpHab 8.1–3),"

same connection that Paul, too, evaluated the suffering of himself and fellow believers as an essential part of the salvation process (e.g., Rom 8:17; Phil 3:10–11).

Joseph Fitzmyer, in particular, showed how something, at least, of the old puzzle about the reference to "the angels" in 1 Cor 11:10 (the praying or prophesying woman ought to "have authority on her head on account of the angels") could be resolved by reference to the Qumran concern to exclude those who were physically blemished from the Community because the holy angels were present in the Community (1QSa = 1Q28a 2.8–9; 1QM 7.6; 4QCD[b] = 4Q267 frag. 17 1.9). Did Paul believe that the unveiled head of a woman was like a bodily defect and share the Qumran belief that Christian gatherings should be conducted "out of reverence for the angels," who are present in such sacred gatherings and who should not look on such a condition?[30]

An amazing number of scholars were early on impressed by the possibility of a relation between the puzzling passage 2 Cor 6:14 – 7:1 and Qumran thought.[31] The Corinthian passage has often been regarded as a non-Pauline insertion, and it was precisely the non- or even anti-Pauline features which seemed to mesh most closely with the thought world of the scrolls. Particularly noticeable here was the call for separation of what is clean from what is unclean,

J. Danielou, *The Dead Sea Scrolls and Primitive Christianity* (Baltimore: Helicon, 1958) p. 100. That a number of NT scholars prefer to read the phrase *pistis Christou* as "the faith(fulness) of Christ" does not greatly weaken the parallel.

30 J. A. Fitzmyer, "A Feature of Qumran Angelology and the Angels of 1 Cor 11:10," *NTS* 4 (1957–58) pp. 48–58; reprinted in his *Essays on the Semitic Background of the New Testament* (London: Chapman, 1971) pp. 187–204; also in Murphy-O'Connor, *Paul and Qumran* pp. 31–47 (here pp. 43–44). For the resultant debate, see D. B. Martin, *The Corinthian Body* (New Haven: Yale University Press, 1995) pp. 243–45.

31 Braun, *Qumran*, vol. 1, pp. 201–4.

whose echoes are obvious. Should this be described as "a Christian exhortation in the Essene tradition," or could it even be that a reworked "Essene paragraph" had been inserted at this point in Paul's letter?[32]

As a final example, we may note that the scrolls have provided the answer to an old conundrum focused on Gal 3:13. In Gal 3:13, the text from Deut 21:23 is cited,[33]— "Cursed is everyone who has been hanged on a tree"—and the text is clearly applied to the crucifixion of Jesus. But equally clearly, the Deuteronomy text refers to the exposure of a criminal after his execution. How could Paul have run the two together? The scrolls have provided the answer: both the Nahum *pesher* and the *Temple Scroll* demonstrate that the language of Deuteronomy had already been referred to the act of crucifixion within the land of Israel. In 4Q169 = 4QpNah 1.7–8, Nah 2:12 is interpreted as referring to "the furious young lion [who executes revenge] on those who seek smooth things and hangs men alive . . ." This is usually taken as a reference to the execution by Alexander Jannaeus of his probably Pharisaic opponents by means of crucifixion. Similarly, in 11QTemple 64.6–13, "hanging on the tree" is understood as a means of execution.[34] The most obvious solution to the conundrum

32   See further V. P. Furnish, *2 Corinthians*, AB 32A (Garden City, NY: Doubleday, 1984) pp. 376–78. The quotations are from J. Gnilka, "2 Cor. 6.14 – 7.1 in the Light of the Qumran Texts and the Testaments of the Twelve Patriarchs," in Murphy-O'Connor, *Paul and Qumran*, pp. 48–66 (here p. 66), and J. A. Fitzmyer, "Qumran and the Interpolated Paragraph in 2 Cor. 6.14 – 7.1," *CBQ* 23 (1961) pp. 271–80, reprinted in his *Essays on the Semitic Background of the New Testament* (London: Chapman, 1971) pp. 205–17 (here p. 217).

33   The textual form has probably been modified to incorporate an allusion to Deut 27:26 and thus to ensure the connection of thought between the curse language of 3:10 and 3:13.

34   See further, particularly J. A. Fitzmyer, "Crucifixion in Ancient Palestine, Qumran Literature and the New Testament," *CBQ* 40 (1978) pp. 493–513, reprinted in his *To*

of Gal 3:13, therefore, is that Paul's use of Deut 21:23 reflects a use of that text in reference to crucifixion, and, quite possibly, in a specific polemical reference to the crucifixion of Jesus.

Comparisons between Qumran and Paul as noted at this earlier phase could readily be multiplied, though several of them would depend on more refined argument. But, hopefully, enough documentation and illustration has been provided to show that potential traffic between the concepts and concerns of the two was considerable, and perhaps in some cases actual. Certainly, the possible links deserve more attention than they have sometimes received.[35]

Of course, at every point, the question has to be asked whether any *direct* influence from one to other is in view, or simply the common influence from the shared heritage of Second Temple Judaism. As ever, "analogy" should not be taken to imply "genealogy." Nevertheless, at the very least, and despite obvious differences in structure and theology, the Qumran Community shared several emphases with Paul—not least, a common sense of absolute dependence on the righteousness of God, of eschatological fulfillment and expectation, and of participation in the elect people and insight into the divine mysteries of God's purpose, with the resultant dualism and disjunction with/within Israel implied. The two groups (Qumran and Pauline Nazarenes) headed in very different directions, but nonetheless, shared heritage and similar starting points mean that the

---

Advance the Gospel: New Testament Studies (New York: Crossroad, 1981) pp. 125–46; O. Betz, "Jesus and the Temple Scroll," in J. H. Charlesworth, ed., *Jesus and the Dead Sea Scrolls* (New York: Doubleday, 1992) pp. 75–103 (here pp. 83–85).

35   Even J. Murphy-O'Connor, "Qumran and the New Testament," in E. J. Epp and G. W. MacRae, eds., *The New Testament and its Modern Interpreters* (Atlanta: Scholars Press, 1989) pp. 55–71, gives little indication of the extent of these potential links (pp. 60–61).

claims and arguments of the one can shed light on those of the other.

II

The second phase relates to the impact of the more recently published scrolls on Pauline studies. This can best be illustrated by reference to the Cave 4 texts, *Songs of the Sabbath Sacrifice* and MMT. In each case, publication of these scrolls has reinforced and consolidated trends in Pauline scholarship which had been given impetus by the earlier scrolls but which had not really succeeded in capturing the frontiers of Pauline research. One has been the trend away from seeking to explain Paul or his churches primarily in Greco-Roman, or more specifically Gnostic terms. The scrolls, given not least the sort of connections outlined above, demonstrated how much of Paul's thought and the issues confronting his churches made good and better sense within the milieu of characteristic Jewish concerns.[36] The other has been the trend to understand Paul's theology as a more nuanced polemic against certain emphases within Second Temple Judaism and not as a complete antithesis to Judaism as such. It can now be said that the scrolls give us a clearer idea of what Paul was objecting to.

The Colossian Philosophy

The first important feature of this second phase of discussion can be neatly focused on the issue of the "Colossian philosophy," that is, what the teaching was which Paul warned his readers against in Colossae. The possibility of Essene influence was long ago raised by J. B. Lightfoot.[37] The dominant view for most of the twentieth century,

---

36   Already Danielou noted how the scrolls showed that "Paul's gnosis in every way is purely Jewish" (*Dead Sea Scrolls*, p. 99).

37   J. B. Lightfoot, *Colossians and Philemon* (London: Macmillan, 1875) pp. 71–111; but at that time the Essenes were "the

however, has been that the Colossian philosophy could only be explained adequately in terms of some more amorphous Jewish-Gnostic syncretism.[38] This line of explanation remains popular and is still being pursued in current studies of the question, with the most recent variations being a kind of "Jewish Pythagoreanism,"[39] "a distinctive blend of popular Platonic, Jewish, and Christian elements that cohere around the pursuit of wisdom,"[40] "a combination of Phrygian folk belief, local folk Judaism, and Christianity,"[41] and "adherents of Cynic philosophy."[42]

What had been missed, and in such theses is still being missed, is the strongly, not to say distinctively Jewish character of the presuppositions shared by Paul and his readers. Some of these had already been observed in the earlier phase of Paul and Qumran discussion. We have already mentioned the prominence of the μυστήριον theme in Colossians 1–3. In addition, the Qumran-like echoes in Col 1:12–13 are particularly striking:[43]

> great enigma of Hebrew history," whose characteristic feature "was a particular direction of mystic speculation, involving a rigid asceticism as its practical consequence . . . we may not unfitly call this tendency Gnostic" (pp. 80–81).

38   Influential here has been the classic commentary by E. Lohse, *Die Briefe an die Kolosser und an Philemon,* KEK 9/2 (Göttingen: Vandenhoeck, 1968).

39   A. J. M. Wedderburn (with A. T. Lincoln), *The Theology of the Later Pauline Letters* (Cambridge: University Press, 1993).

40   R. E. DeMaris, *The Colossian Controversy: Wisdom in Dispute at Colossae,* JSNTSup 96 (Sheffield: Sheffield Academic, 1994).

41   C. E. Arnold, *The Colossian Syncretism,* WUNT 2.77 (Tübingen: Mohr-Siebeck, 1995).

42   T. W. Martin, *By Philosophy and Empty Deceit: Colossians as Response to a Cynic Critique,* JSNTSup 118 (Sheffield: Sheffield Academic, 1996).

43   See Flusser, "The Dead Sea Sect and Pre-Pauline Christianity" in *ScrHie* 4, pp. 30–1; Braun, *Qumran,* p. 226. The parallels were also noted by Lohse, *Kolosser,* pp. 69–71.

> Col 1:12 — God "has qualified you for the share of the inheritance of the holy ones in the light."

> 1QS 11.7–8 — "God has given them (wisdom, knowledge, righteousness, power, and glory) to his chosen ones as an everlasting possession and has caused them to inherit the lot of the holy ones."

> 1QH 19(formerly 11).10–12 — "For the sake of thy glory thou hast purified man of sin that he may be holy for thee . . . that he may be one [with] the children of thy truth and partake of the lot of thy holy ones."

The continuation of the thought in Colossians in terms of a light/darkness dualism (". . . the inheritance of the holy ones in the light. He has delivered us from the authority of darkness and has transferred us into the kingdom of the son of his love," Col 1:12–13) equally resonated with the Qumran dualism between "the sons of light" and "the sons of darkness" already noted (1QS 1.9–10; 3.24–25; 4.7–13; 1QM e.g., 1.1, 8–14; 13.5–16).

What was insufficiently appreciated, however, was the extent to which this passage typified a characteristically Jewish perspective on the blessings brought by the gospel and of the perils from which such Gentile believers had escaped.[44] The same feature is evident in the positive evaluation of circumcision and disparagement of "the uncircumcision of your flesh" (Col 2:11, 13) which is so distinctively Jewish. In such circumstances, it is more likely to be an intensification of the Jewish appeal of the Colossian philosophy rather than the dilution of its Jewishness which was the problem for Paul. And this indeed is what we find in the allusion to the appeal of this alternative system in Col 2:16 and 22, where it is clear that the Colossian Christians

44   For what follows, see further my "The Colossian Philosophy: A Confident Jewish Apologia," *Biblica* 76 (1995) pp. 153–81.

were being faulted for their failures in regard to food and festivals, including the Sabbath, and purity laws.[45]

The issue has focused on Col 2:18[46] with its puzzling reference to an opponent "who delights in humility and the worship of angels, which things he had seen on entering." The possibility, even likelihood of Qumran shedding light on this had already been mooted at an earlier stage,[47] and indeed had been gaining strength in the scholarly debate.[48] But what I regard as a decisive contribution to the debate has been given by the publication of the *Songs of the Sabbath Sacrifice*. For here we have not only confirmation that the Qumran Community saw itself as a priestly community whose holiness was defined by the presence of the angels (1QH 11[formerly 3].21–22; 19[formerly 11].10–13). More to the immediate point, we have confirmation of 1Q28b = 1QSb 4.25–26 that the Community saw its worship as somehow sharing in the worship offered by the angels. And most interesting of all, we have examples of the songs of praise to

45   The parallels with Galatians at this point (particularly Gal 4:9–10 and Col 2:8, 16) have not been given sufficient attention. As W. Schenk observes, calendar piety, food laws, and circumcision cannot be regarded as random elements of some syncretistic cult, but are the very norms which provide and confirm the identity of Israel ("Der Kolosserbrief in der neueren Forschung (1945–85)," *ANRW* 2.25.4 (1987) pp. 3327–64 (here pp. 3351–53).

46   Cf. particularly C. E. Arnold, *The Colossian Syncretism*, p. 10, whose central thesis is that the "worship of angels" (Col 2:18) "refers essentially to a magical invocation of angels, especially for apotropaic purposes."

47   See Braun, *Qumran*, vol. 1, pp. 231–32.

48   Particularly F. O. Francis, "Humility and Angel Worship in Colossae," in F. O. Francis and W. A. Meeks, eds., *Conflict at Colossae* (Missoula: Scholars Press, 1973) pp. 163–95; and T. J. Sappington, *Revelation and Redemption at Colossae*, JSNTSup 53 (Sheffield: Sheffield Academic, 1991). Note also L. T. Stuckenbruck, *Angel Veneration and Christology*, WUNT 2.70 (Tübingen: Mohr-Siebeck, 1995) pp. 111–19.

be offered to God by angels in the heavenly temple, with the clear implication that the Qumran Community itself joined with the angels in reciting these songs of heavenly worship, while recognizing their unworthiness to do so.[49] Moreover, we also have a clarification of the otherwise puzzling talk of "entering" ("things seen on entering"). For in the context thus illuminated, the talk of "entering" is most obviously explained by reference once again to 4Q405 with its talk of doorways to the heavenly temple (presumably based on Ezekiel 40–41)[50] and theme of entering (4Q405 14–15i.3–4 and 23i.8–10).[51]

In short, the Dead Sea Scrolls have shown how plausible it is to understand the Colossian philosophy as a form of distinctively Jewish mystical worship practiced in the Colossian synagogue, which was very similar in character to the worship so valued at Qumran, and which gave the Colossian Jews a sense of superior privilege by reference to which claims of the Gentile Christians could only be disqualified and dismissed.

Works of the Law

The other trend in Pauline scholarship was signaled by the work of E. P. Sanders and its aftermath, usually indicated by the phrase, "the new perspective on Paul."[52] Sanders

49   C. Newsom, *Songs of the Sabbath Sacrifice: A Critical Edition* (Atlanta: Scholars Press, 1985) particularly pp. 59–72; cf. Stuckenbruck, *Angel Veneration*, pp. 156–61.

50   Newsom, *Songs*, pp. 39–59.

51   The *Songs of the Sabbath Sacrifice* can also shed light on the element of mysticism in Paul's own writings, implied in 2 Cor 12:1–4 and perhaps also in 2 Cor 2:14 and the use of Ps 68:18–19 in Eph 4:8; see J. M. Scott, "Throne-Chariot Mysticism in Qumran and in Paul," in C. A. Evans and P. W. Flint, eds., *Eschatology, Messianism, and the Dead Sea Scrolls* (Grand Rapids: Eerdmans, 1997) pp. 101–19.

52   E. P. Sanders, Paul and Palestinian Judaism (London: SCM, 1977); J. D. G. Dunn, "The New Perspective on

showed how different was the Judaism of the time from the stereotyped Christian view of Jewish legalism. The fact that Judaism in all its principal expositions was a religion of covenant grace, dependent on Temple sacrifice for sin and divine forgiveness, was by no means a new insight, but it took the polemical demonstration of Sanders for the point to be properly registered—despite the fact, already noted, that the Qumran Scrolls gave poignant expression to that same basic reliance on divine grace.

This recognition of the essential similarity between Christian gospel and Jewish precedent, however, posed still more sharply the question: If Paul was not objecting to Jewish legalism, to what was it that he opposed his doctrine of justification by faith? The answer obviously lay in the phrase which Paul sets in antithesis to justification by faith—that is, justification by "works of the law." But that phrase, "works of the law," seemed to be a distinctively Pauline phrase, and it raised the question as to whether Paul had coined it himself and had a peculiar or jaundiced view of the Judaism from which he had turned. It was surprisingly late in the day that notice was taken of the appearance of the same phrase or its near equivalent in the scrolls, particularly 4Q174 (Flor) 1.7—"He has commanded that a sanctuary of men be built for himself, that there they may send up, like the smoke of incense, the works of the law."[53]

Paul," *BJRL* 65 (1983) pp. 95–122, reprinted in my *Jesus, Paul and the Law: Studies in Mark and Galatians* (London: SPCK, 1990) pp. 183–214.

53   The earliest reference I am aware of is by D. J. Moo, "'Law,' 'Works of the Law,' and Legalism in Paul," *WTJ* 45 (1983) pp. 73–100 (here p. 91). Earlier discussion by K. Kertelge, "Zur Deutung des Rechtfertigungsbegriffs im Galaterbrief," *BZ* 12 (1968) pp. 211–22, reprinted in his *Grundthemen paulinischer Theologie* (Freiburg: Herder, 1991) pp. 111–22, continued to cite as the nearest parallel 2 Bar 57:2 (Str-B 3.160), and noted only the similar phrases "works of righteousness" (1QH 1.26; 4.31) and

It is at this point that the impact of 4QMMT has been most clearly felt. The fact that a document was soon to be published which contained the precisely equivalent phrase, מעשי התורה was widely trailed before the publication of MMT.[54] But its publication in 1994[55] revealed astonishing links into Pauline thought. In the final section of the document, three points of contact became immediately apparent with Paul's language and line of thought in Galatians in particular.[56]

The first is the self-description of the writer(s) of the scroll: "we have separated ourselves from the multitude of the people [. . .] and from being involved with these things and from participating with [them] in these things" (Qimron C7–8). What is so striking is that this seems to be the first occurrence of that phrase, "separated ourselves from," and that it matches the accusation made by Paul against Peter at Antioch so precisely—Peter (and the other Christian Jews) "separated himself" from the Christian Gentiles in Antioch, having previously eaten with them (Gal 2:12). In each case, we have one section of a larger community separating itself from the rest, presumably over purity issues, to avoid "participating with them." In other words, the attitude and concerns which Paul condemned at Antioch are the attitude and concerns by which MMT expressed and justified the establishment of the Qumran Community.

"doers of the law" (1QpHab 7.11; 8.1). Surprisingly Kuhn, "Impact," p. 330, seems to have been unaware of 4QMMT; so too H.-J. Eckstein, *Verheissung und Gesetz: Eine exegetische Untersuchung zu Galater 2.15–4.7*, WUNT 86 (Tübingen: Mohr, 1996).

54   See e.g., my *Romans*, WBC 38 (Dallas: Word, 1988) p. 154.
55   E. Qimron and J. Strugnell, *Miqsat Maʿase Ha-Torah*, DJD 10, p. 5.
56   In what follows, I draw upon my "4QMMT and Galatians," *NTS* 43 (1997) pp. 147–53.

The second striking point of contact is, of course, the occurrence of the key phrase itself מקצת מעשי התורה "some of the works of the law": "And also we have written to you some of the works of the Torah which we think are good for you and for your people" (C26–27; García Martínez, pp. 112–13).[57] The allusion back to the beginning of the second section of the text is beyond dispute: "These are some of our rulings [. . .] which are [. . .] the works which w[e consider . . ." (B1–2). What then follows is a series of halakhic rulings, chiefly relating to the Temple, priesthood, sacrifices and purity, and regularly introduced with the formula, "we consider that" or "we say that" (B8, 29, 36, 37, 42, 55, 73). In other words, "the works of the law" in MMT denote the obligations which the Qumran leadership considered to have been laid upon them by the Torah, the requirements of the Torah as understood or interpreted in the Qumran Community. It follows also that these "works of the law" were precisely the reason why the Qumranites considered it necessary to "separate themselves" from the rest of Israel: "the works of the Torah" so understood could not be (properly) observed otherwise.

Again, the parallel with Galatians is striking. For the sequence of thought in Gal 2:12–16 makes it clear that Peter and the other Christian Jews would have justified their action in separating themselves from the larger Christian community in Antioch by a precisely analogous appeal to "the works of the law" (Gal 2:16). Here, too, the phrase summarizes a series of Torah requirements, particularly circumcision (Gal 2:1–10) and the rules governing table-fellowship with Gentiles (2:11–15), which a body of Jews believed it to be essential that they should observe, essential, presumably, as part of their covenant obligation as

---

57   F. García Martínez has revised the translation of his first edition, "the precepts of the Torah" (following Qimron C27), to the more obvious "the works of the Torah," cf. *The Dead Sea Scrolls Translated: The Qumran Texts in English* (Leiden: Brill, 1994,[2] 1996) p. 79.

members of Israel. In other words, when Paul denied so emphatically that justification was by works of the law (Gal 2:16), he almost certainly had in mind the same attitude which we find expressed in 4QMMT.

The third striking point of comparison between Galatians and MMT is the way in which appeal is made to the formulation which goes back to Gen 15:6—"he (the Lord) reckoned it (Abraham's faith[fulness]) to him as righteousness." In MMT, the appeal is made to the recipients of the letter that they find "some of our practices/rulings are correct/true" (C30, my translation).[58] And the letter immediately continues: "And it will be reckoned for you as righteousness when you perform what is right and good before him, for your own good and for that of Israel" (C31–32). Here, evidently, the reckoning of righteousness is a consequence of doing "the works of the Torah."[59] In Galatians, by way of contrast, Paul cites Gen 15:6 to prove that justification is by faith (as in the case of Abraham) and *not* by works of the law. In other words, Paul uses precisely the same formula, and alludes to precisely the same precedent of Abraham, but does so to refute precisely the same logic and argument which we find in MMT.[60]

What is so impressive in this case is the coincidence of three such striking parallels within such brief compass. One might be an accident, two a coincidence, but three make it hard to doubt that the language and rationale expressed in both documents reflect an essentially similar attitude

58   The phrase "some of our rulings" is precisely the same as that used in B1, and is evidently equivalent to the key phrase "some of the works of the Torah."

59   For similar allusions to Gen 15:6, see Ps 106:31; 1 Macc 2:52; *Jub* 30.17.

60   The point was already observed by M. Abegg, "Paul, 'Works of the Law' and MMT," *BARev* 20 (1994) pp. 52–55, 82. In contrast, the contributors to J. Kampen and M. J. Bernstein, eds., *Reading 4QMMT: New Perspectives on Qumran Law and History* (Atlanta: Scholars Press, 1996) fail to notice the link.

and self-understanding. But this means that, for the first time, we have a document which expresses just the self-understanding within Judaism and among Jews to which Paul reacted so fiercely. Which is also to say that what Paul was objecting to, in that which is still generally regarded as his most central and characteristic teaching, was not the product of his idiosyncratic career or his fevered imagination but an understanding of God's righteousness and grace and their consequences which were very familiar in the Qumran Community. It was not the grace of God which Paul found lacking in his fellow Christian Jews. It was the corollary which they drew which he could no longer stomach: that recipients of this grace had to observe works of the law which separated them from others, whether other Jews or other Christians. On this key point of Pauline (and so also Christian) theology, Qumran has indeed shed new light on Paul.

In summation, these two features have, in my judgment, confirmed and made irreversible the trend and need to set Paul's theology firmly within a Jewish context. This is neither to affirm much, if any, direct influence from Qumran to Paul; nor is it in any way to deny the influence of Hellenistic thought, particularly Paul's awareness and use of popular Greek philosophy and rhetoric. But if we are to enter into the warp and woof of Paul's theology, it is its essentially Jewish content and character with which we must reckon most fully. And, in this respect, the light shed on Paul from Qumran has been and continues to be invaluable and irreplaceable.[61]

61   I am grateful to my colleague, Loren Stuckenbruck, for his helpful comments on the first draft of this paper.

Index of Authors

Abegg M. G. 62n16, 126n60
Albani, M. 64n23
Albright, W. F. ix-xi, xii, 76
Alexander, A. 11n15
Alexander, H. S. 63nn19, 21,
  64n22
Allegro, J. M. 42n8, 56n1,
  62n18
Arav, R. 77n1
Arnold, C. E. 119n41, 121n46

Attiridge, H. W. 93n16
Audet, J. P. 21n3

Baillet, M. 72n47
Bar Adon, P. 33n31
BarthJlemy, D. 3n1, 5nn5, 7,
  11n16, 12
Baumgarten, I. A. 26n20,
  27n23
Baumgarten, J. M. 69n41,
  70n43
Baumgartner, W. xivn7
Beal, S. 23n9
Beit-AriJ, M. 9
Benoit, P. 108n9, 110n18,
  113n24
Berger, K. 84n9
Bernstein, M. 49n20, 57n3,
  60n12, 70n42, 126n60
Betz, O. xin4, 101n23,
  117n34
Beyer, K. 64n24, 70n43,
  72n48
Bianci, U. 57n4
Bickerman, E. 14n20
Black, M. 66n28, 107n8
Boccaccini, G. 49n23, 52n35

Bockmuehl, M. N. A.,
  113n25
Braun, H. 105, 106nn4,7,
  109nn14-15, 110n17,
  110n20, 111nn21-23,
  115n31, 119n43, 121n47
Brooke, G. 49n22
Broshi, M. 24n12, 25n16,
  26n19, 28n24, 35n38,
  111nn23
Brown, R. E. 113n24
Brownlee, W. xi, 1, 76
Burchard, C. 36n40
Burrows, M. xi, 56n1, 107n8

Caquot, A. 69n38
Chambon, A. 25n14, 26n19
Charlesworth, J. H. 46n16,
  50n24, 57n5, 68n37, 78n2,
  82n7, 93n16, 100n21,
  101n24, 105n2, 108n12,
  111n23, 117n34
Collins, J. J. 39n1, 91n14,
  93n16
Coppins, J. 113n24
Cross, F. M. xin4, 2, 5n4,
  36-37, 40-41, 76
Crown, A. 31n32

Daniel, G. 35n37
Danielou, J. 115, 118n36
Davies, W. D. 107n7
Dayagi Mendels, M. 50n24
De Boer, P. A. H. 9n12
De Rossi, J. B. 7
De Vaux, R. xiii, xivn7, 21n6,
  25n14, 25nn17, 19, 36n39,
  39-40
Diest, F. 17n25

Dimant, D. 22n8, 26n19, 65n25, 72n47, 106n3
Donceel, R. 28
Donceel-Vofte, P. 28, 29nn27-28, 39
Duhaime, J. 58n5, 59n9
Dunn, J. D. G. 122n52
Dupont-Sommer, A. 56n2

Eades, K. 9n13, 12n21
Eckstein, H.-J. 124n53
Eliade, M. 57n4
Epp, E. J. 117n35
Erasmus, D. 10
Eshel, H. 24n12, 25n16, 27n23, 28n24
Evans, C. A. 72n49, 83n7, 91n14, 122n51

Feldman, L. H. 82n4
Fishbane, M. 44n13
Fitzmyer, A. J. 115n30, 116n32,34
Flint, P. W. 67n33, 91n14 , 122n51
Flusser, D. 95n19, 105, 106n4, 107n7, 109n13, 111n23, 113n26, 119n43
Fox, M. 22n8
Francis, F. O. 121n48
Freedman, D. N. 62n16, 76
Freund, R. A. 77n1
Frey, J. 58nn5-6, 59n9
Furnish, V. P. 116n32

G@rtner, B. 114n27
Gammie, J. G. 57n5
GarcRa-MartRnez, F. 30n30, 36n40, 48n20, 49n20, 50n24, 52nn33-34, 56n1, 57n3, 70n42
Ginsburg, C. D. 7
Gitin, S. 35n38

Gleuck, N. 35n36
Gnilka, J. 116n32
Golb, N. 21n5, 29n29, 31n31, 39n1
Goodman, M. 24n13
Goshen-Gottstein, M. 3n1, 9n12, 13, 11n15, 12nn17-18, 17n26
Greenfield, J. C. 64n23, 65nn27-28
Greenspoon, L. 16n24

Haas, N. 31n31
Hachilili, R. 27n22
Haran, M. 22nn7-8
Harding, L. xivn7
Horowitz, W. 65n26, 66n28
Huggins, R. V. 69n37
Humbert, J. B. 25n14, 26n19
Hurvitz, A. 62n16

Ivry, S. 32n35

Johns, L. L. 101n24
Jongeling, B. 36n40

Kahle, P. 11n15
Kampen, J. 49n20, 57n3, 70n42, 87n10, 87n10, 126n60
Kapera, Z. J. 31n31
Kennicott, B. 7
Kertelge, K. 108n11, 123n53
Klinzing, G. 114n27
Knohl, I. 62nn16-17
Kuhn, H.-W. 106n3, 108n10, 110n19, 124n53
Kuhn, K. G. 56n2, 107n7

Lange, A. 57n3, 58n7, 70n42, 44
Lichtenberger, H. 58n5
Lightfoot, J. B. 118n118

Lohse, E. 119n38,43
Luther, M. 10

Magness, J. 25n15, 29nn25-26
Marcus, D. 16n24
Maris, R. E. 119n40
Martin, D. B. 115n30,
    125n57
Martin, T. W. 119n42
McRae, G. W. 117n35
Meier, J. P. 82n6
Merrill, E. H. 23n9
Michaelis, J. D. 11
Milik, J. T. 48n19,
    61nn14-14, 67n32, 69n37,
    69n41, 71n45
Moo, D. J. 123n53
Murphy-O'Connor, J. 108n9,
    113n24, 115n30, 116n32,
    117n35
Mussner, F. 113n24

Nathan, H. 31n31
Netzer, E. 25n18
Newsom, C. 122n50
Newton, M. 114n28
Nida, E. 3
Nizan, B. 72n47

Olson, D. T. 61n13

Pardee, D. 39n1
Parry, D. W. 24n12, 36n40,
    100n21
Pike, S. H. 35n38
Porter, S. E. 72n49
Puech, I. 48n20, 71n47,
    72n48

Qimron, E. 87n10, 108n12,
    124n55

Rabin, C. 3n1
Rackman, H. 20
Rappaport, U. 26n19, 72n47,
    106n3
Reich, R. 24n12
Revell, E. J. 9n12
Riesner, R. 101n23
Roberts, B. J. 9n12
Roberts, J. J. M. 68n37

Samuel, A. Y. xii-xiii, 75
Sanders, E. P. 122n52
Sanders, J. A. 4n2, 8n8, 9n13,
    11n14, 14n21, 76
Sappington, T. J. 121n48
Schenk, W. 121n45
Schick, A. xin4, xiin5, xivn7
Schiffman, L. 22n8, 27n21,
    40n2, 50n25, 56n1, 65n25
Schmidt, F. 63n20
Schult, H. 32n34
Scott, J. M. 122n51
Segal, M. 42n9
Seifrid, M. A. 108n10
Shaked, S. 56n2
Shavit, Y. 22n7
Skehan, P. W. 2
Sokoloff, M. 64n23, 65n27
Spinoza, B. 10
Steckroll, S. 25n19
Stegemann, H. 49n22, 51n29
Stendahl, K. 105, 107nn7-8
Stern, M. 21n4
Stone, M. E. 56n1
Strugnell, J. 62n18, 87n10,
    124n55
Stuckenbruck, L. T. 121n48
Stulmacher, P. 108n11
Sukenik, E. L. 19
Sukenik, E. xiii
Sun, H. 9n13, 14n21

Tal, A. 16n24

Talmon, S. 3n1, 5n4, 12n19, 13, 16n23, 60n12, 62nn18-17, 83n7

Talshir, Z. 16n24

Taylor, J. E. 82n5, 83

Tolbin, T. H. 93n16

Tov, E. 3n1, 4n5, 5n5, 8n8, 12n19, 16n23, 40n2, 42nn8-9, 43n10, 44n11

Trebolle Barrera, J. 46n15, 48n20, 56n1, 66n29, 67n32

Trever, J. ix-x, xi, 1, 76

Ulrich, E. 24n12

Van der Woude, A. 30n30, 67n32

VanderKam, J. 40n2, 41n5, 45n15, 48n19, 56n1, 70n45, 88n11

Vegas Montaner, L. 46n17, 48n20, 67n32

Vermes, G. 41n6, 56n1, 106n6

Von der OstenSacken, P. 57n3

Wacholder, B. Z. 51n28, 62n16, 66n29

Wedderburn, A. J. M. 119n39

Werblowsky, Z. 57n4

White-Crawford, S. 42n8, 43n10, 44n11

Wills, L. 50n24

Wilson, A. M. 50n24

Winston, D. 56n2

Wintermutte, O. S. 46n16, 47n18

Wise, M. O. 22n7, 31n31, 39n1, 39n1, 50n24, 51nn30-32, 64n23, 65n27

Wright, P. D., 62n16

Yadin, Y. 19n1, 23nn10-11, 48n20, 49n21, 50n26, 75, 100n22

Zissu, B. 26n20

Index of Scripture References

(Includes Tanakh, Deuterocanonical, and New Testament)
References to an entire book are not included.

Genesis 1 – Exodus 12   **45**

Genesis
12:10–20   46
15:6   126
20:2–7   46
27:45   48
28:5   47
28:6   47

Exodus 4:11   **69**

Leviticus
15:14–15   43
18:25–29   43
19:1–4   43
19:9–15   43
24:2   44, 50

Deuteronomy
21:23   116 – 117
27:26   116
32:39   69

1 Samuel 5:6   **69**

2 Samuel 22   **15**

Isaiah
40   82, 83
40:3   80, 82 – 83, 101
58   94
61   94

Ezekiel 40–41   **122**

Nahum 2:12   **116**

Habakkuk
2:2   112
2:4   114

Psalms
18   15
51   89
68:18–19   122
106:31   126
155:11   93

Proverbs 15:8   **113**

Daniel 9   **67**

Baruch 53   **68**

1 Maccabees 2:52   **126**

Tobit 5:18–22   **48**

Matthew
3:3   83
3:5   87
3:7–10   86
3:12   87
5:44   98
10:30   97
12:11   97
12:49–50   94
15:10–20   97
19:12   95

Mark
1:5   87
2:1–12   78
3:34–35   94
7:14–23   97

Luke
1:5–25   86
1:57–80   86
1:80   86
3:3   87
3:4   83

Luke (cont.)

3:7–9	86
3:10–14	86 – 87
3:17–18	87
4:1	94
4:2	94
4:21	94
8:21	94
10:25–37	98
12:7	97

John

1:23	83
1:29–42	82
3:22	90
3:22–24	82
4:1	82, 90
4:2	82, 90
13:34	98

Romans

1:16–17	108
1:17	114
2:12–16	108
3:20	108
3:20–26	106
3:21 – 4:25	114
7:7–25	110
7:22–23	110
8:6	110
8:15	111
8:17	115
9:15–23	111
12:1	113
13:12–13	111

1 Corinthians

2:12	109
3:16–17	114
6:11	109
11:10	115
12:10	111
12:13	109
13	98
14:12	111

2 Corinthians

2:14	122
3:6	109
6:14 – 7:1	115
12:1–4	122

Galatians

2:1–10	125
2:11–15	125
2:12	124
2:12–16	125
2:16 – 3:29	114
2:16	125 – 126
3:10	116
3:11	114
3:13	116 – 117
4:4–5	109
4:6	109
4:9–10	121
5:5	108

Ephesians

2:18–22	114
3:3	113
3:5	113
4:8	122
5:8–14	111

Philippians 3:10–11   **115**

Colossians

1:12	120
1:12–13	119 – 120
1:25–26	112
1–3	119
2:8	121
2:11	120
2:13	120
2:16	120 – 121
2:18	121
2:22	120

1 Thessalonians

4:8	109
5:4–8	111

Index of Ancient Manuscripts and Works

11Ps[a] 27.6–7   60

11Q17   60

11QPs[a] (11Q11)   67, 71
4.7–9   72

11QTemple
21.12–28   60
23–24   50
64.6–13   116

1Q28b = 1QSb 4.25–26   121

1QH
1.24   67
1.26   123
4.17   109
4.26   109
4.31   123
9.21   112
10.13   112
11.21–22   121
12.27   112
12.29–30   106
15.6–7   109
19.10–13   121
19.10–12   120

1QM
1.1, 8–14   120
2.6, 8   68
7.6   115
13.5–16   120
13.9–14   111

1QpHab
7   94
7.3–5   112
7.11   124
7.13   67
8.1   124
8.1–3   114

1QpHab (cont.)
9.1–2   69
9.10–12   69

1QS
1–2   98
1.9–10   120
2.23–25   89
2.8   89
3–4   59,110
3.13   56,60
3.13 – 4.14   109
3.13 – 4.26   23,87,108,110
3.15   67
3.15 – 4.1   111
3.18–26   60
3.19   110
3.22–23   60
3.22–24   71
3.24–25   120
3.25   110
3.6–8   109
3.6–8 – 4.21   109
4.12   69
4.12–14   71
4.13   67
4.15–16   60, 111
4.15–17   110
4.21   109
4.23   110
4.23–24   110
4.23–25   111
5.5ff.   114
5.13–14   85
7.3   23
8.4ff.   114
8.13–14   82
9.3ff.   114
9.4–5   113
10–18   89
10.1–2   60
11.7–8   120
11.9–15   107

1QS^a = 1Q28^a
1.4–5   24
1.9–10   24
2.8–9   115

4Q169
= 4QpNah 1.7–8   116

4Q174 (Flor) 1.7   **123**

4Q180   **68 - 69**
1.1–2   60

4Q181   **68 - 69**

4Q186   **62 - 64,66,87**
1 ii 7–9   63

4Q208–211   **61**

4Q247   **67**

4Q258   **58**

4Q259   **58**

4Q266
6 i   69
6 i 6   69
6 i 12   69

4Q269 7   **69**

4Q272 1 i   **69**

4Q273 4 ii   **69**

4Q318   **64 - 65**

4Q320   **61**

4Q320–330   **60**

4Q321   **62,65 - 66**

4Q322   **66**
4 4,6   66

4Q324^a 2   **67**

4Q331   **60**

4Q334   **60**

4Q364   **47**

4Q365   **43 - 44,50 - 51**

4Q367   **43**

4Q381
24 6   93
46 5   93

4Q390   **67**
1   67

4Q394
(4QMMT^a) 1–2 I-v 1–16   60

4Q400–407   **60**

4Q403
1 25–26   94
1 i 1   94
1 i 32   94

4Q405
14–15i.3–4   122
23i.8–10   122

4Q496
(4QMf) frg. 7, line 3   68

4Q503   **61,65**

4Q510–511   **71 - 72**

4Q513 frg. 18, line 3   **68**

4Q534   **64**

4Q560   **70**

4QCD^b
= 4Q267 frag. 17 1.9   115

4QFlor   **114**

4QMMT   **87,124–126**
See also 4Q394.

4QpHos ii 15–17   **60**

4QvisAmrb
   (4Q544) ii 1–6 iii 1–2   72

1 Enoch
   10.5–6   72
   15.8–12   71
   37–71   91
   72–76   61, 65
   75.01   66
   84–90   67
   89.54–90   68
   91   67
   91.10–17   68
   93   67
   93.1–10   68

Damascus Document
   See Also 4Q266.
   2.9–10   67
   3.13–16   60
   6.18–19   60
   6.19   109
   7.6–9   24
   8.21   109
   10.8–10   46
   11.20–21   113
   11.13   97
   13.3   63
   16.3–4   46
   19.33–34   109

Genesis Apocryphon
   20.16, 28–29   69

Jubilees   **46**
   1.14   60
   6.23–38   60
   10   71
   10.9   71
   12   46
   16.3–4   68
   27   47
   27.14   47
   27.17   47
   30.17   126

Masada ShirShabb ii 7   94

Rule of the Community
   See 1QS.

Temple Scroll
   See 11QTemple.

Testament of Levi 16 67–68

Index of Greek, Hebrew, and Aramaic Words and Phrases

Greek

ἀγαθὸν ἄνδρα	81
ν τῇ ῥήμῳ	82
μυστήριον	119
πεπλήρωται	94
σήμερον	94

Hebrew and Aramaic

deber	69
genizah	19
pesher	94, 99, 109, 114, 116
shemṭot	68
ruaḥ	63
yaḥad	84, 88–89, 94

47	אותו תראה
47	אחרי יעקוב בנה
108	אמת
95	בית קודש
82	במדבר
107	בצדקת אל
107	בצדקת אמתו
107–108	חסד
82	למדבר
94	מל ותו
94	מל מלא ים
124	מעשי התורה
125	מקצת מעשי התורה
107–108	משפט
107	משפטי
107–108	צדקה
95	קדשים
96	קדושי קודש קודשים
95	קודש קודשים
95	רוח קודש
47	תראה בלום